North America
Time for a New Focus

COUNCIL *on*
FOREIGN
RELATIONS

Independent Task Force Report No. 71

David H. Petraeus and
Robert B. Zoellick, *Chairs*
Shannon K. O'Neil, *Project Director*

North America
Time for a New Focus

The Council on Foreign Relations (CFR) is an independent, nonpartisan membership organization, think tank, and publisher dedicated to being a resource for its members, government officials, business executives, journalists, educators and students, civic and religious leaders, and other interested citizens in order to help them better understand the world and the foreign policy choices facing the United States and other countries. Founded in 1921, CFR carries out its mission by maintaining a diverse membership, with special programs to promote interest and develop expertise in the next generation of foreign policy leaders; convening meetings at its headquarters in New York and in Washington, DC, and other cities where senior government officials, members of Congress, global leaders, and prominent thinkers come together with CFR members to discuss and debate major international issues; supporting a Studies Program that fosters independent research, enabling CFR scholars to produce articles, reports, and books and hold roundtables that analyze foreign policy issues and make concrete policy recommendations; publishing *Foreign Affairs*, the preeminent journal on international affairs and U.S. foreign policy; sponsoring Independent Task Forces that produce reports with both findings and policy prescriptions on the most important foreign policy topics; and providing up-to-date information and analysis about world events and American foreign policy on its website, www.cfr.org.

The Council on Foreign Relations takes no institutional positions on policy issues and has no affiliation with the U.S. government. All views expressed in its publications and on its website are the sole responsibility of the author or authors.

The Council on Foreign Relations sponsors Independent Task Forces to assess issues of current and critical importance to U.S. foreign policy and provide policymakers with concrete judgments and recommendations. Diverse in backgrounds and perspectives, Task Force members aim to reach a meaningful consensus on policy through private and nonpartisan deliberations. Once launched, Task Forces are independent of CFR and solely responsible for the content of their reports. Task Force members are asked to join a consensus signifying that they endorse "the general policy thrust and judgments reached by the group, though not necessarily every finding and recommendation." Each Task Force member also has the option of putting forward an additional or dissenting view. Members' affiliations are listed for identification purposes only and do not imply institutional endorsement. Task Force observers participate in discussions, but are not asked to join the consensus.

For further information about CFR or this Task Force, please write to the Council on Foreign Relations, 58 East 68th Street, New York, NY 10065, or call the Communications office at 212.434.9888. Visit CFR's website at www.cfr.org.

This report is printed on paper that is FSC® Chain-of-Custody Certified by a printer who is certified by BM TRADA North America Inc.

MIX
Paper from
responsible sources
FSC® C101537

Task Force Members

Task Force members are asked to join a consensus signifying that they endorse "the general policy thrust and judgments reached by the group, though not necessarily every finding and recommendation." They participate in the Task Force in their individual, not institutional, capacities.

Bernard W. Aronson
ACON Investments

Jodi Hanson Bond
U.S. Chamber of Commerce

Robert C. Bonner*
Sentinel HS Group, LLC

Jason Eric Bordoff*
Columbia University

Timothy P. Daly
Western Union

Jorge I. Domínguez
Harvard University

Stephen E. Flynn
Northeastern University

Gordon D. Giffin
McKenna Long & Aldridge LLP

Neal R. Goins
Exxon Mobil Corporation

Kenneth I. Juster
Warburg Pincus LLC

Marie-Josée Kravis
Hudson Institute

Jane Holl Lute
Council on CyberSecurity

Jason Marczak
Atlantic Council

Diana Natalicio
University of Texas at El Paso

Shannon K. O'Neil
Council on Foreign Relations

Maria Otero*
Independent Consulting

James W. Owens
Caterpillar Inc.

David H. Petraeus
KKR Global Institute

*The individual has endorsed the report and signed an additional or dissenting view.

This report is dedicated to the memory of Task Force member Robert A. Pastor, a visionary champion of the North American idea, who passed away during the course of this effort.

Contents

Foreword

The United States, Canada, and Mexico are bound by a shared geography, history, and environment. In the twenty years since the passage of the North American Free Trade Agreement, the continent's three economies and societies have become deeply intertwined, making relations between the United States and its immediate neighbors more important than ever.

In 2005, in conjunction with counterpart organizations in Canada and Mexico, the Council on Foreign Relations published *Building a North American Community*, which proposed the establishment of a North American economic and security community by 2010, the boundaries of which would be defined by a common external tariff and an outer security perimeter. Nearly a decade since the report's release, its bold vision is still mostly a distant goal.

Many of the issues facing North American policymakers in 2005 remain: growing global economic competition, uneven development within North America, and threats to mutual security. New and welcome trends have also emerged, however: significant increases in energy production in the United States and Canada, an increasingly confident Mexico bolstered by political and economic reforms, and a decline in migration from Mexico to its northern neighbors.

This report of the CFR-sponsored Independent Task Force on North America examines both the long-standing issues facing the region and more recent developments, urging policymakers to elevate and prioritize the North American relationship.

The Task Force's recommendations focus on four pivotal areas: capitalizing on North America's promising energy outlook by removing restrictions on energy exports and increasing investment in infrastructure; bolstering economic competitiveness through the freer movement of goods and services across borders; strengthening security through a unified continental strategy and support for Mexico's efforts to solidify democratic rule of law; and fostering a North American community through comprehensive immigration reform and the creation of a mobility accord to facilitate the movement of workers. The Task Force makes the case that a revitalized North American partnership is good not just for local reasons but also because it will strengthen the position of the United States and the continent in the world.

I would like to thank the Task Force's chairs, David H. Petraeus and Robert B. Zoellick, for their decisive leadership, expert guidance, and continued dedication to producing a comprehensive report. I also extend my thanks to the distinguished group of Task Force members and observers, whose diverse backgrounds and expertise helped shape this report.

I am grateful to Christopher M. Tuttle, who took on this project as the new director of CFR's Independent Task Force Program and whose contributions have been instrumental to the Task Force process. I would finally like to thank Project Director and Senior Fellow for Latin America Studies Shannon K. O'Neil for undertaking a project of this scope and expertly incorporating the many perspectives represented by the Task Force to create a report that is intended to remind the American people that our country's most important relationships remain close to home.

Richard N. Haass
President
Council on Foreign Relations
October 2014

Acknowledgments

The report of the Independent Task Force on North America is the product of much work and effort by the dedicated members and observers of the Task Force, and I am deeply appreciative of the time and expertise they have lent to this project.

In particular, I thank our distinguished chairs, David H. Petraeus and Robert B. Zoellick, for their firm leadership, thoughtful guidance, and steadfast dedication throughout the course of the Task Force. It has been a privilege to work with and learn from both of them. I also thank the members of their staffs, particularly Maile Trenholm and Sharada Strasmore, for their help throughout this process.

Many Task Force members and observers offered detailed comments and feedback throughout the writing process, for which I am deeply appreciative. Special thanks go to Robert C. Bonner, Stephen E. Flynn, Neil R. Goins, Jane Holl Lute, Michael A. Levi, and Edward Alden, as well as to outside readers Rafael Fernández de Castro and Stephen Kelly.

The chairs and I had the fortunate opportunity to travel to Canada and Mexico in January for consultations that informed this report, and we are thankful to the number of individuals who met with our delegation. We benefited greatly from briefings by current and former government officials in Ottawa and Mexico City, as well as representatives from the private sector, civil society, and press. The Task Force delegation is also grateful to the many Canadian and Mexican officials who offered their time and insights, as well as U.S. ambassador E. Anthony Wayne and chargé d'affaires ad interim Richard M. Sanders and their respective staffs. Special thanks to Claudio X. Gonzalez and Rafael Fernández de Castro in Mexico and John P. Manley, Eric Miller, and Colin Robertson in Canada for their help in facilitating a number of these meetings.

We also received helpful input from many CFR members. The Washington Meetings team organized an event in Washington, DC, which I led with Task Force member Clifford Sobel; the New York Meetings team held an event for CFR members in New York; and the Corporate Program organized a briefing for executives, which I led with Task Force member Jodi Hanson Bond.

My gratitude goes to CFR's Publications team for editing the report and readying it for publication, as well as CFR's Communications, Corporate, National, Outreach, and Washington teams for ensuring that the report reaches the widest audience possible. Additionally, CFR's Events teams in New York and Washington deserve thanks for ably coordinating all of the Task Force's meetings.

Chris Tuttle and Veronica Chiu of CFR's Independent Task Force Program were instrumental to this project from beginning to end, from selecting Task Force members to convening meetings to editing multiple drafts of the report. I am grateful to them for their support and for keeping the project on track. My research associate, Stephanie Leutert, deserves much credit and thanks for her research and assistance with the report, as does her successor, Gilberto Garcia, for shepherding the report to final publication. I also extend my thanks to Anya Schmemann and Kristin Lewis for their help in launching this Task Force at the outset.

I am grateful to CFR President Richard N. Haass and Director of Studies James M. Lindsay for giving me the opportunity to direct this project.

Once again, my sincere thanks to all who contributed to this effort.

Shannon K. O'Neil
Project Director

Acronyms

APEC	Asia-Pacific Economic Cooperation
ARI	Advanced Resources International
ASEAN	Association of Southeast Asian Nations
ATF	Bureau of Alcohol, Tobacco, Firearms, and Explosives
BECC	Border Environment Cooperation Commission
BRIDGE	Building and Renewing Infrastructure for Development and Growth in Employment Act
CAFTA-DR	Central American-Dominican Republic Free Trade Agreement
CBP	Customs and Border Protection
CDC	Centers for Disease Control and Prevention
CEC	Commission for Environmental Cooperation
CERTs	Computer Emergency Readiness Teams
CESOP	Centro de Estudios de Opinión Pública
COOL	country of origin labeling
C-TPAT	Customs-Trade Partnership Against Terrorism
CUSFTA	Canada-United States Free Trade Agreement
DHS	Department of Homeland Security
DOE	Department of Energy
EIA	Energy Information Administration
EPA	Environmental Protection Agency
EU	European Union
FAST	Free and Secure Trade
FDA	Food and Drug Administration

FERC	Federal Energy Regulatory Commission
FVEY	Five Eyes
FY	fiscal year
G20	Group of Twenty
G7	Group of Seven
GAO	Government Accountability Office
GDP	gross domestic product
HLRCC	U.S.-Mexico High-Level Regulatory Cooperation Council
IBETs	Integrated Border Enforcement Teams
ICE	Immigration and Customs Enforcement
IDB	Inter-American Development Bank
IDENT	Automated Biometric Identification System
IMCO	Instituto Mexicano para la Competitividad (Mexican Competitiveness Institute)
IMF	International Monetary Fund
LNG	liquefied natural gas
NADB	North American Development Bank
NAFTA	North American Free Trade Agreement
NALS	North American Leaders' Summit
NATO	North Atlantic Treaty Organization
NORAD	North American Aerospace Defense Command
NORTHCOM	United States Northern Command
OECD	Organization for Economic Cooperation and Development
PAHO	Pan American Health Organization
Pemex	Petróleos Mexicanos
PISA	Programme for International Student Assessment
PNWER	Pacific Northwest Economic Region
PPPs	public-private partnerships
RCC	U.S.-Canada Regulatory Cooperation Council
SENTRI	Secure Electronic Network for Travelers Rapid Inspection

SPP	Security and Prosperity Partnership of North America
TN	Treaty NAFTA
TPP	Trans-Pacific Partnership
TTIP	Transatlantic Trade and Investment Partnership
USCIS	U.S. Citizenship and Immigration Services
US-VISIT	United States Visitor and Immigrant Status Indicator Technology
WTO	World Trade Organization

Task Force Report

Executive Summary

North America was once called the New World. The people, their ideas, and the resources of the continent shaped the histories of the Old World—East and West. Today, North America is home to almost five hundred million people living in three vibrant democracies. If the three North American countries deepen their integration and cooperation, they have the potential to again shape world affairs for generations to come.

For reasons of history and political culture, the United States, Canada, and Mexico are each highly protective of national sovereignty and independence. Yet twenty years ago, the three countries instituted a novel project to deepen integration while respecting sovereignty. Moreover, their special partnership bridged the North-South divide between developed and developing economies. The North American Free Trade Agreement (NAFTA) has been the cornerstone of this new structure. The new post–Cold War North America was conceived as an integrated economy within a global system, not as a protected bloc or experiment in shared sovereignty, as was the case with the European Union.

Recent developments have created opportunities for the North American countries to build on past work and to advance their partnership to a new stage. There is a fundamental shift in the continent's energy outlook, driven by technology, innovation, investment, and new policies. In addition, Mexico's ambitious structural reform agenda is creating prospects for higher growth, an expanding middle class, and a better-educated and more productive workforce. North America's demographics are healthier than Europe's, China's, Japan's, and Russia's. These factors, combined with higher costs in other regions of the world and the ability of the U.S. private sector to seek out technological frontiers, are pulling global investors to North America. North America has the potential to become a new type of growth market, combining the best of cutting-edge developed-economy innovation with the best of developing country structural reforms.

Over the past twenty years, the international perspectives of the three North American democracies have converged, especially on economic topics, but potentially on challenges of security, rule of law and transnational crime, hemispheric development, and the environment. Yet most regional issues and irritants, though important, rarely rise to the urgency of international crises. Canadians and Mexicans are frustrated that the United States does not treat its neighborhood as a priority. North America has been an afterthought of U.S. policy.

The Task Force believes it is time for U.S. policymakers to put North America at the forefront of a strategy that recognizes that North America should be the "continental base" for U.S. global policy.

The U.S. government faces a structural challenge in pursuing such a continental policy. The diversity of federal agencies involved and the vital roles of state and local governments, legislatures, and myriad private actors make it hard to fashion a comprehensive policy. *The Task Force recommends creating new North American offices within the National Security Council staff and U.S. State Department to focus responsibility for the development and execution of continental policies, catalyze and support cooperation at different levels of government, and insert a North American perspective into U.S. discussions of global policies.*

The Task Force also recommends that one of the senior-most U.S. officials assume responsibility as North America's "champion." And national policy needs to encourage and facilitate state, provincial, local, and legislative leaders in the identification of problems, solutions, and opportunities. North America requires a new type of transnational foreign policy.

U.S. policy toward North America should prioritize cooperation on energy, economic competitiveness, security, and the issues of a common community. The guiding framework should be: trilateral where we can, bilateral where we must.

ENERGY

The innovation, investment, and increased production in the energy sector is already giving North America a global competitive advantage. Yet continental energy and environmental policies are not keeping up. *The Task Force recommends specific steps to strengthen the continental energy infrastructure (including approval of the Keystone XL pipeline), expand energy exports, support Mexico's historic reforms, secure safety, and encourage harmonized policies to promote energy conservation and lessen carbon costs.* The North American countries need a regional energy strategy.

ECONOMIC COMPETIVENESS

Since the passage of NAFTA, North America has vastly expanded its internal trade and investment. The continent has moved closer to becoming a joint innovation, design, production, and service platform. As a result, the United States, Canada, and Mexico have become more efficient and competitive together. Living standards have improved.

Nevertheless, a combination of border policies, gaps in infrastructure, resistance to competition and structural reforms, and opportunities elsewhere have slowed momentum toward a truly competitive North American market. The trilateral economic relationship needs an upgrade to meet twenty-first-century requirements. *The Task Force recommends specific steps to achieve the free and unimpeded movement of goods and services across North America's internal borders.*

Improvements in North America's transportation networks, expansions of preclearance programs, and a focus on expediting logistics and value chains could boost regional growth and assist all three countries in competing globally. North America is not using its technological edge to interconnect its national economies securely and efficiently. *The Task Force recommends moving toward a border management goal of "cleared once, approved thrice."*

U.S. trade and global economic policies need to recognize trilateral economic interests. The continent operates increasingly as an economic unit with interconnected interests. The Trans-Pacific Partnership (TPP) negotiations, in which all three North American countries participate, could be used to upgrade old NAFTA provisions. *The Task Force calls for Canada and Mexico to be included in the U.S. negotiations with the European Union for a Transatlantic Trade and Investment Partnership (TTIP), so as to foster continental integration and outlook.* NAFTA also opened the door to closer economic linkages between North and Latin America. *The Task Force recommends that the North American countries explore how to build on overlapping free trade agreements (FTAs)—such as the Pacific Alliance and U.S. and Canadian bilateral FTAs with Latin American countries—to move toward freer trade for the Western Hemisphere.*

SECURITY

North America has come a long way from the wars of the nineteenth century. Its 7,500 miles of borders reflect stress points from new risks, but the absence of territorial disputes and spirit of cooperation are the envy of powers around the world.

To gain the full benefits of continental integration, the North American partners need to face common threats together. Terrorists, criminal and narcotics organizations, cyberattacks, and disease pose dangers to all three. *The Task Force recommends working toward a long-term goal of a unified security strategy for North America.* This process could begin by expanding bilateral security programs trilaterally.

The United States and Canada also have a shared interest in helping Mexico strengthen its rule of law and combat organized crime. *The Task Force recommends that the United States, in conjunction with Canada, build on the Mérida Initiative to support Mexican efforts to strengthen the democratic rule of law, dismantle criminal networks, contribute to the development of resilient and cohesive communities, and reduce arms smuggling and drug consumption.*

North Americans also need to act as one to face broader regional security challenges. *The Task Force calls for consideration of a new North American and regional effort to assist Central America along the lines of Plan Colombia; the United States and Canada should also develop a common Arctic strategy.*

COMMUNITY

The people of North America are critical to the future of a competitive, healthy continent. Indeed, the individuals and families of North America are its most vital resource. Unlike much of the rest of the world, the demographics of North America could be another source of strength. To capitalize on this possibility, the three countries need to encourage the development of an educated, skilled, flexible, mobile, and shared workforce. The education sector is facing a transformative moment; vast possibilities are opening up through innovative use of technologies, new models of schooling, and competitive cost pressure for tertiary education. Each North American country will preserve local prerogatives for education, but they can also learn from and cooperate with one another.

The Task Force strongly recommends the passage of comprehensive federal immigration reform that secures U.S. borders, prevents illegal entry, provides visas on the basis of economic need, invites talented and skilled people to settle in the United States, and offers a pathway to legalization for undocumented immigrants now in the United States. The Task Force also recommends the creation of a North American Mobility Accord, an expansion and facilitation of the Treaty NAFTA (TN) visas for skilled workers, streamlined recognition of professional credentials, and the development of a regional educational innovation strategy.

The people of North America are creating a shared culture. It is not a common culture, because citizens of the United States, Canada, and Mexico are proud of their distinctive identities. Yet when viewed from a global perspective, the similarities in interests and outlooks are pulling North Americans together.

The foundation exists for North America to foster a new model of interstate relations among neighbors, both developing and developed democracies. Now is the moment for the United States to break free from old foreign policy biases to recognize that a stronger, more dynamic, resilient continental base will increase U.S. power globally. "Made in North America" can be the label of the newest growth market. U.S. foreign policy—whether drawing on hard, soft, or smart power—needs to start with its own neighborhood.

Introduction: The Importance of North America

North America has always been both a land apart and a feature within a larger global system. For Europeans, North America was a "New World," a strange frontier where British, French, Spanish, and Russian empires collided with one another and with indigenous peoples, who themselves had migrated from Asia long before. In the late eighteenth and nineteenth centuries, the descendants of these explorers, settlers, and soldiers—reinforced by immigrants from all quarters of the globe—created their own new nation-states. These states clashed over the territory and control of North America, shaping its political destiny. A strong sensitivity to national sovereignty in all three North American countries is the legacy of these struggles. Over time, the nations developed a respect and even a fondness for their neighbors, though there has been some lingering wariness about the dominance of the United States.

In the twentieth century, North America, the continental outpost beyond the great Eurasian expanse, became both an Atlantic and a Pacific power. The United States and Canada grew closer as they recognized that their similarities and shared global interests outweighed their differences. Near the end of the century, Mexico, which had maintained a working but distant relationship with the United States, made a courageous decision—to look north, to forge new economic links with the United States and Canada. In doing so, Mexico fused North and Latin America.

The new post–Cold War North America was conceived as an integrated economy within a global system, not as a protected bloc. The United States, Canada, and Mexico—in different ways—sought to combine close North American ties with global interconnections. The three New World states of North America once again stood apart as a region; economies increasingly integrated through the North American Free

Trade Agreement, even as they also assumed individual roles within a rapidly changing world order.

There have been many studies about North American, U.S.-Mexican, U.S.-Canadian, and even Mexican-Canadian relations, including some by the Council on Foreign Relations (CFR). That valuable work has usually been the province of regional specialists. Our aim, as a Task Force, was to consider North America from a different vantage point— a global perspective. For reasons we will discuss, we believe that the time is right for deeper integration and cooperation among the three sovereign states of North America.

Here is our vision: three democracies with a total population of almost half a billion people; energy self-sufficiency and even energy exports; integrated infrastructure that fosters interconnected and highly competitive agriculture, resource development, manufacturing, services, and technology industries; a shared, skilled labor force that prospers through investment in human capital; a common natural bounty of air, water, lands, biodiversity, and wildlife and migratory species; close security cooperation on regional threats of all kinds; and, over time, closer cooperation as North Americans on economic, political, security, and environmental topics when dealing with the rest of the world, perhaps focusing first on challenges in our own hemisphere.

In sum, we recommend a new partnership for North America, a new model for the world of integration and cooperation among sovereign states. The foundation for U.S. foreign policy in years to come should be "Made in North America."

The Task Force believes that North America should be a central priority for U.S. policy. North America is the "continental base" for the United States; it should be the starting point for its geopolitical and geoeconomic perspectives. The development and implementation of a strategy for U.S. economic, energy, security, environmental, and societal cooperation with its two neighbors can strengthen the United States at home and enhance its influence abroad.

Building on the experience of the North American Free Trade Agreement, the United States, Canada, and Mexico can develop a modern model of integration that both respects sovereign prerogatives and demonstrates the mutual benefits of deeper cooperation. Moreover, this endeavor would establish the potential of closer partnership between developed and developing economies.

WHY NOW?

Several recent developments make a North American vision particularly attractive. Most important, there has been a fundamental shift in North America's energy landscape. New finds and increased production in the United States and Canada—and very likely Mexico in the years ahead—are altering economic calculations, energy flows, and global geopolitics. Advances in the energy arena create enormous possibilities as well as some challenges, all of which can be better dealt with by the three nations acting together.

North America can capitalize on other opportunities as well. The combination of rising labor costs in China, as well as energy and transportation expenses, lengthy travel times to and from Asian factories, and worries about poor intellectual property protections offer compelling reasons for manufacturing firms and other businesses to shift production to North America. *The Task Force believes U.S. policies to promote deeper economic and energy integration, facilitating regional supply chains, will encourage investment in North America.*

Reforms in Mexico are also generating increased interest in North America. Mexico has drawn closer to its two northern neighbors since NAFTA entered into force in 1994. The Mexican economy, once led by agriculture and commodities, now relies heavily on manufacturing and services. Mexico's politics have evolved from one-party rule to a truly competitive democracy. And Mexico's society is increasingly shaped by a solid middle class with expanded links around the world.

As Mexico has changed, so too has its relationship with the United States, and to a lesser extent Canada. Through the integration of production, movement of people, expanded connections across the Pacific, and shared security challenges, these three nations have drawn closer in outlook. Their interests have become inextricably linked. The Enrique Peña Nieto administration's recently launched, hugely ambitious reform agenda—covering education, telecommunications, energy, taxation, and governance—should improve Mexico's productivity and further open Mexico to its neighbors and the world. At the same time, the threats of rising violence have aligned Mexican and U.S. interests and spurred the development of joint strategies to address transnational criminal threats.

Now is also an auspicious time to deepen U.S. ties with Canada. Canada's political leadership and its public support greater regional integration but have been frustrated by the lack of U.S. attention. According to a survey by American University's Center for North American Studies, EKOS Research Associates, and the Centro de Estudios de Opinión Pública (CESOP), more than half of all Canadians support closer cooperation with their North American neighbors.[1]

North America also connects three of the world's most far-reaching efforts to liberalize trade and investment. The Trans-Pacific Partnership aims to combine roughly 40 percent of the world's gross domestic product (GDP) in a comprehensive free trade agreement. The Transatlantic Trade and Investment Partnership seeks to link the United States and the European Union (EU) through free trade and regulatory cooperation. Depending on their terms, both accords could enhance North American dynamism and competitiveness. The Pacific Alliance—founded by Mexico, Colombia, Peru, and Chile in 2012—will extend Latin American cooperation beyond free trade to financial and diplomatic issues; this partnership has the potential to transform outlooks across the region. The expansion of the Panama Canal could boost the region's role in the global economy as well.

The Task Force recognizes that the United States, Canada, and Mexico have an opportunity to enhance their global influence by strengthening their continental base while respecting each country's national sovereignty.

NORTH AMERICA: AN AFTERTHOUGHT FOR U.S. POLICYMAKERS

The U.S. pursuit of a North American policy has been limited because many regional issues and irritants, though important, rarely rise to the urgency of international crises. The Task Force believes that U.S. policymakers should make North America a pillar of U.S. foreign policy. *To reverse a pattern of inattention and the treatment of these relations as an afterthought, the United States should make an ongoing investment in North American policies.*

Responsibilities for North American policy are scattered across the U.S. government, making it harder to fashion a comprehensive policy. The regional bureaus at the U.S. Department of State and U.S. embassies have the primary responsibility for coordinating activities with countries around the world. However, accountability for the development and execution of North American policies is far more diffuse.

Almost every "domestic" agency in the U.S. government—ranging from the Department of Transportation to the Social Security Administration—plays an important role in dealing with the country's North American neighbors. *The Task Force believes a coherent North American strategy will require leadership to guide more systematic engagement among federal agencies—and also to work with state and local governments, private sectors, and civil societies—in all three countries.*

Although it recognizes the common interests and interconnections among the three North American partners, the Task Force is also well aware of major differences among them. Each has a unique history, domestic sensitivities, and political culture. Mexico, in particular, has a substantial income gap with its northern neighbors. Deep disparities also exist between levels of safety and quality of education.

The countries' foreign policies differ as well. Canada and the United States share long-standing institutional ties, including membership in the North Atlantic Treaty Organization (NATO), the Group of Seven (G7), Five Eyes (FVEY) intelligence cooperation, and the North American Aerospace Defense Command (NORAD).[2] Canadians fought alongside U.S. troops in Afghanistan, losing 158 lives. Mexico, on the other hand, has been less involved with its neighbors' foreign policies and on the world stage; indeed, it has been a reluctant, wary partner in past foreign and security policy endeavors. Mexico's constitution enshrines a foreign policy doctrine of "nonintervention," keeping the nation outside of many noneconomic multilateral institutions. In addition, Mexican and Canadian policymakers have often preferred to protect special, bilateral relationships with the United States, rather than develop tripartite associations.

Nevertheless, the differences in international outlook among North America's countries are much smaller today than they were twenty years ago; they will likely be smaller still twenty years from now. The three countries work well together in the Group of Twenty (G20), World Trade Organization (WTO), International Monetary Fund (IMF), World Bank, Inter-American Development Bank (IDB), and Organization for Economic Cooperation and Development (OECD). The differentiation among the three countries can also present opportunities for cooperation in different roles.

In practice, however, bilateral approaches continue to dominate. On some issues, at least in the near term, more progress may be made through one-on-one negotiations. But shared concerns and interests are often overlooked in these narrower interactions, leading to failures to capitalize on the longer-term benefits of working together.

PAST EFFORTS

The last serious attempt to deepen North American ties and develop a common agenda was in 2005, when U.S. president George W. Bush, Mexican president Vicente Fox, and Canadian prime minister Paul Martin formed the Security and Prosperity Partnership of North America (SPP). The SPP established a trilateral dialogue supported by working groups on issues such as transportation, financial services, the environment, and intelligence cooperation. It also created an annual leaders' summit.

Some thought the SPP reached too far. It linked local and domestic security and economic concerns to continent-wide policies, provoking reservations over a supposed loss of sovereignty. It engaged business leaders in the three countries to define and develop concrete initiatives to further trilateral ties through the North American Competitiveness Council. In retrospect, the SPP's scope was too limited. The partnership brought the North American leaders together each year, but not much occurred between the summits. The lack of institutional mechanisms for follow-through hampered the implementation and advancement of proposed policies and programs. Furthermore, the absence of legislative branch and broader civil society involvement heightened suspicions and left out many who could have helped deepen cooperation.

In 2009, the countries downgraded the SPP to the North American Leaders' Summit (NALS). The NALS does not have any standing committees; instead, it acts as a platform for recommendations and pledges. The private sector–led North American Competitiveness Council was disbanded. Meetings between North American cabinet-level administrators now occur on a sporadic and ad hoc basis. Senior officials often have a limited mandate and are not able to coordinate effectively across various stakeholder or governmental interests to solve problems. As a result, busy officials do not devote consistent attention to North American issues.

Nevertheless, some coordinated, institutionalized efforts have advanced. The three central banks work together to ensure stable and liquid financial markets. The three nations share passenger, flight, and other information to keep out potential criminals and terrorists. They also cooperate in the face of natural disasters. The Commission for Environmental Cooperation (CEC), created under NAFTA, has invested successfully in a handful of important projects that foster regional environmental conservation and protection.

But these modest efforts will not provide the foundation for a true North American transformation. They will not move regional cooperation and integration from an afterthought to a priority. In fact, the continued reliance on bilateral efforts—such as the U.S.-Canada Beyond the Border initiative and the U.S.-Mexico High Level Economic Dialogue—inhibits the development of a broader vision of North America.

Because of geography, markets, and the choices of millions of individuals and thousands of companies, North America has become one of the most integrated and interdependent regions in the world. Sharing 7,500 miles of peaceful borders, Canada and Mexico now play vital roles in the United States' stability, security, and prosperity. There is, however, substantial unfulfilled potential. The region deserves much more attention. *The Task Force believes that today's challenge is to envisage a North American vision, frame a concept of North American policy aims and cooperation, and make this policy agenda a priority.* A stronger North America will enhance U.S. competitiveness, security, and well-being and bolster U.S. influence globally. The United States should invest in its home region to forge a stronger continental base for the twenty-first century.

North American Energy Interdependence

North America's energy landscape is changing dramatically. In 2005, net imports made up 60 percent of U.S. oil consumption. The growing gap between the United States' energy demand and domestic supply added to worries about the U.S. trade deficit, economy, and security.[3] Today, U.S. oil import dependence has dropped to less than 40 percent of total consumption, and the country is shifting rapidly from energy scarcity to opportunity. Rising unconventional oil and gas production in the United States, increasing exploration and development in the Canadian oil sands, and landmark reforms in Mexico's energy sector have led many experts to predict the potential—especially with North American natural gas—for self-sufficiency and even surplus in the coming decades. The growing production and regional diversification of energy sources will boost North America's energy security and competitiveness.

The decisions the United States, Canada, and Mexico make about energy will have major implications for their economies, national security, foreign policy, and environment. Reliable, affordable, and environmentally sustainable energy production can strengthen each country and also North America as a whole. If combined with energy efficiency, this new energy landscape can bolster the region's economic base and provide new opportunities for leadership.

INCREASING ENERGY PRODUCTION

As a result of technological advances, abundant reserves, high oil prices, a receptive investment climate, and solid infrastructure, the United States' oil and gas production has boomed over the past decade (Figures 1 and 2). Hydraulic fracturing—commonly known as fracking— along with advances in seismic technology and directional (horizontal)

FIGURE 1: NORTH AMERICAN CRUDE OIL PRODUCTION
(1980–2013)

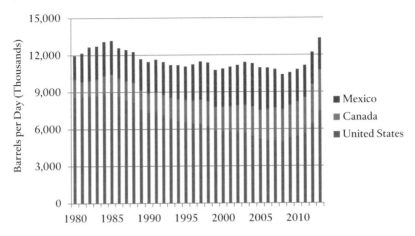

Source: U.S. Energy Information Administration (EIA).

FIGURE 2: NORTH AMERICAN DRY NATURAL GAS PRODUCTION
(1980–2012)

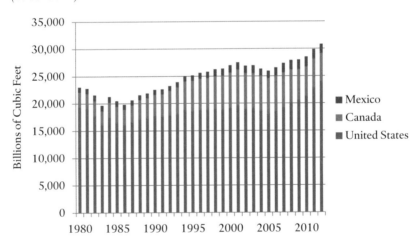

Source: U.S. EIA.

drilling, are enabling oil and gas extraction from low-porosity and low-permeability rock, boosting U.S. crude oil output to its highest level in two decades. Just this year, the United States surpassed Saudi Arabia to become the top oil and natural gas liquids producer in the world (Figures 3 and 4).[4]

FIGURE 3: DRY NATURAL GAS PRODUCTION BY COUNTRY (2012)

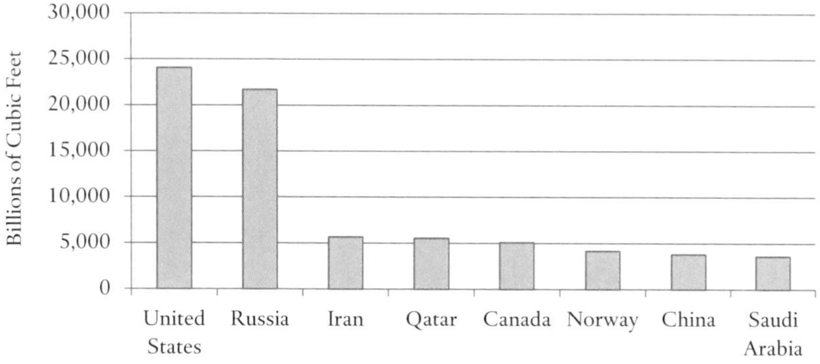

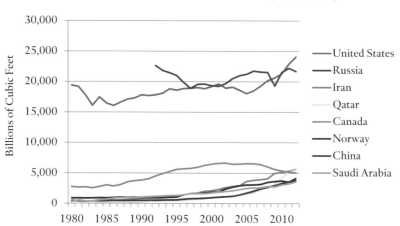

Source: U.S. EIA.

FIGURE 4: DRY NATURAL GAS PRODUCTION (1980–2012)

Source: U.S. EIA.

The increase in U.S. natural gas production has been just as dramatic, rising from eighteen trillion to twenty-four trillion cubic feet since 2005, making the United States the largest natural gas producer in the world.[5] The United States looks forward to the prospect of further increases in the years ahead.

Canada's oil production is also growing rapidly. According to the Energy Resources Conservation Board, production of crude bitumen has tripled since 2000 and is expected to reach 3.8 million barrels per day (b/d) by 2022.[6] The U.S. Energy Information Administration estimates that Canada's less-developed shale gas fields contain the world's fifth-largest reserves.[7] And both the United States and Canada will likely benefit from newly accessible fields in the Arctic, which are estimated to account for nearly a quarter of the world's undiscovered oil and gas resources.

In contrast, Mexican oil production has fallen nearly 25 percent since 2004 to 2.5 million b/d in 2012. The downturn reflects the declining output at Cantarell—once the world's second-largest oil field—combined with lower-than-expected production levels in newer fields, such as the Chicontepec Basin. The decline can also be traced to underinvestment, inefficiencies, and limits on technology and expertise at the state-owned energy company Petróleos Mexicanos (Pemex). Nevertheless, Mexico's energy potential is substantial. The EIA and Advanced Resources International (ARI) estimate that the country has the world's sixth-largest recoverable shale gas resources and significant tight oil potential.[8]

Mexico has now made a historic move: its energy reform of December 2013 will encourage private companies to invest in Mexico's energy sector for the first time since the 1930s. The government hopes its new policies will attract capital, technology, and skills to boost oil and gas production. Depending on the final structure of the auctions and contracts, Mexico's Ministry of Finance and Public Credit estimates that foreign investment could help lift oil production 40 percent by 2020.[9] The reform also opens up the country's electricity grid to private competition, creating the prospect of important reductions in Mexico's high prices for electricity.

Finally, North American renewable energy—including wind, solar, hydro, and biofuels—adds even more capacity to the region's optimistic energy forecast.[10] North America is already the world's largest biofuel producer, accounting for nearly half of global ethanol and biodiesel production in 2013.[11] Solar energy is developing rapidly as well, and steadily declining costs are making the technology increasingly competitive against traditional energy sources.[12] Wind power has also gained market share; Texas breezes now power some 3.3 million households and new Mexican projects are positioning the country to become one of the fastest-growing markets in the world.[13] These energy sources are still largely dependent on subsidies, but technological advances and declining costs may boost their ability to compete against traditional energy sources in the years to come.

ENERGY INTEGRATION

As production grows, North American energy security would be strengthened by continental integration. Canada is already the United States' largest supplier of oil and petroleum products, accounting for one-third of total U.S. oil imports. For many years, virtually all of Canada's energy exports—including oil, gas, and electricity—went to the United States. In turn, the United States sent north a small amount of crude oil and a more sizable amount of refined petroleum products.[14] Overall, the bilateral energy trade reached close to $134 billion in 2013, or more than 20 percent of the two countries' total trade.[15]

The United States and Mexico are also close energy partners. In 2013, Mexico sent 85 percent of its crude oil exports north—equaling 850,000 b/d—making Mexico the United States' third-largest oil supplier, behind only Canada and Saudi Arabia.[16] In the same year, the United States sent some $20 billion in petroleum products south, bringing the two countries' energy exchanges to nearly $60 billion, roughly 11 percent of total bilateral trade.[17] Growing energy production in the United States, increasing demand in Mexico, and U.S. refining capacity suited for Mexico's heavy crude help sustain a robust bilateral energy relationship.[18] The United States' ratification of the Transboundary Hydrocarbon Agreement in December 2013, which states guidelines for exploring and developing shared deep-water oil fields in the Gulf of Mexico, will deepen ties further.

Natural gas is also widely exchanged within North America, flowing between the United States, Canada, and Mexico through forty-eight pipelines—with more pipelines and greater volumes to come. Virtually all of Canadian natural gas exports are sent south, supplying more than

10 percent of the United States' total gas consumption in 2013.[19] Rising U.S. domestic production has displaced some of these flows; indeed, since 2007, U.S. natural gas exports to Canada have almost doubled, while Canadian exports to the United States have declined. These shifts pose challenges for the two trading partners.

U.S. natural gas exports to Mexico have been expanding rapidly— almost doubling from 2010 to 2012. These exports are expected to increase even more, due to growing Mexican demand and added infrastructure.[20] New pipelines under construction will be crucial to boosting this trade, starting with the 750-mile-long Ramones Pipeline that will connect Agua Dulce, Texas, to Mexico's central industrial area. Expected to come online at the end of 2015, the Ramones Pipeline will tap into Texas' Eagle Ford shale gas output and could potentially carry nearly a fifth of Mexico's natural gas needs.[21]

The North American countries are also connected through their electricity grids; this is especially true for the United States and Canada. The Eastern Interconnection grid—encompassing parts of Eastern Canada, New England, and New York—and the Western Interconnection grid—stretching from Manitoba through the U.S. Midwest—are mutually dependent and beneficial configurations. Though the U.S.-Canada electricity trade constitutes less than 2 percent of total U.S. domestic consumption, the interchanges provide resiliency in case of power overloads or natural disasters. U.S.-Mexico interconnections are more limited, though the two countries are linked in southern California and southwestern Texas.

BROADER ECONOMIC EFFECTS

The role of energy in each North American economy varies substantially (Figure 5). Canada's growing oil and gas production has pushed energy products up to almost a quarter of the country's exports—surpassing traditional Canadian industries such as automobile manufacturing. By comparison, Mexico's oil and gas industry has shrunk as a share of the overall economy. Thirty years ago, oil made up 70 percent of Mexico's exports and around 20 percent of GDP. Today, oil is closer to 15 percent of Mexican exports and less than 10 percent of GDP (though royalties and taxes still make up roughly one-third of Mexico's federal government budget). In the United States, the oil and gas sector

FIGURE 5: NORTH AMERICAN OIL RENTS (PERCENTAGE OF GDP)

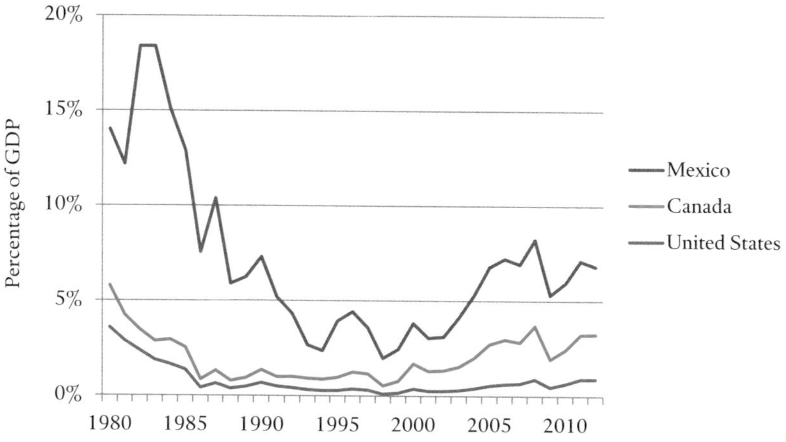

Source: World Bank.

remains a small part of the overall U.S. economy and employment base, though the recent expansion in the U.S. energy industry has led to significant direct and indirect benefits for consumers, communities, and energy-intensive industries.

North America's oil and gas industry is the most obvious and largest beneficiary of the recent boom. In 2012, the region's investment in exploration and production totaled more than $250 billion. IHS, an energy analysis and forecasting firm, calculates that the outlays could grow to more than half a trillion dollars annually by 2016.[22]

Companies that supply this burgeoning sector benefit significantly, including those that provide materials for oil and gas wells and those that house, feed, and clothe the expanding workforce. More broadly, the lower cost of natural gas is changing the financial calculations for many companies that use natural gas as a raw material or source of low-cost energy. Energy- and natural gas–intensive industries such as petrochemicals, cement, glass, fertilizer, aluminum, plastics, and steel—composing some 7 percent of the U.S. industrial sector—benefit the most. The energy cost advantage, coupled with factors such as wages, productivity, and exchange rates, has reduced overall U.S. manufacturing costs, which are now notably lower than almost all major competitors.[23]

Workers are benefiting from the energy boom, too, though economists disagree on the extent and permanence of these positive trends.
The largest employment effects have occurred within the oil and gas
industry, which, according to Goldman Sachs, has created 175,000 jobs
since 2010 as a result of the shale revolution.[24] By 2020, companies in
this sector will likely have added even more jobs over the previous
eight years; estimates range from 110,000 (McKinsey) to 190,000
(IHS) to 550,000 (Citi).[25] When adding indirect and induced jobs—
those in the energy supply chain or marginally related to the oil and
gas industry—the estimates rise to between roughly one and two million new jobs by 2020.[26]

Although important, these positions still make up less than 1 percent of
the United States' total employment. In U.S. manufacturing, the oil and
gas boom may have simply halted job losses in energy-intensive industries, as opposed to leading to an increase in employment.[27] The ultimate
number of jobs created will depend on the size of the U.S. energy industries, overall employment in the U.S. economy, and the breadth of job
types included in the counting. Whatever the actual effects, growing oil
and gas production represents an important economic bright spot.

Similar trends are emerging in Canada and Mexico. Nearly two hundred thousand Canadian workers are employed directly in the upstream
and midstream oil sectors, and this number is expected to increase by
9 to 20 percent over the next decade.[28] The Mexican Competitiveness
Institute (IMCO), a well-regarded think tank, predicts that Mexico's
energy reform, if fully implemented, will create more than three hundred thousand direct, indirect, and induced new jobs a year.[29]

Finally, lower natural gas prices are passed along to consumers as
they heat their homes and water, turn on the lights, and purchase every-
day goods. IHS calculates that the average U.S. household saved some
$1,200 in 2012 for a total of $163 billion in annual consumer gains.[30]
There will be further savings in the future.

ENVIRONMENTAL EFFECTS

The increase in North American oil and gas exploration and production could pose trade-offs for the environment. The clearing of
forests, potential contamination of groundwater, and large-scale oil
spills, such as that seen in the 2010 Gulf of Mexico *Deepwater Horizon*

incident, can be devastating for residents and ecosystems. Increased carbon emissions contribute to global climate change. Although there are important areas of uncertainty, climate change poses serious risks. These changes could impose large costs on agricultural, energy, insurance, and other sectors.

U.S. carbon emissions have fallen to levels last seen in the mid-1990s, when the economy was much smaller than it is today. Overall, U.S. and Canadian energy consumption per capita has declined (Figure 6). The shifting makeup of fossil fuels has also lowered emissions, replacing coal with natural gas for power generation. Energy efficiency has helped as well, especially in the transportation sector, where energy consumption per person is expected to continue decreasing.

SECURING ECONOMIC BENEFITS WHILE PROTECTING THE ENVIRONMENT

To date, most of the economic growth and benefits from the new energy boom have come from upstream activities, including indirect and induced jobs.[31] To capture more extensive benefits, the North American

FIGURE 6: TOTAL PRIMARY ENERGY CONSUMPTION PER CAPITA (1980–2011)

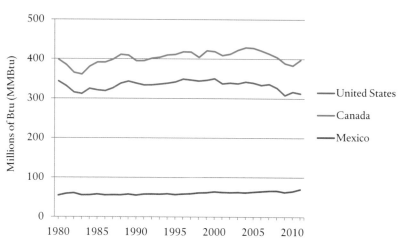

Source: U.S. EIA.

countries should clarify the uncertainties that are limiting downstream investment, which is usually capital intensive and long-lived.[32] The United States, Canada, and Mexico should establish credible, stable, clearly defined regulatory and policy frameworks for integration and cooperation on energy issues across national borders. To be sustainable, such policies should encourage growth and development while addressing environmental and carbon concerns.

The Task Force finds that North America should reap the full benefits of its energy bounty. To do so, the three countries should clarify uncertainties by developing credible, sustainable policy frameworks for responsible North American energy development that encourage growth while addressing significant environmental issues.

GEOPOLITICAL EFFECTS

Gas markets are less global than oil markets, leading to significant price differentials across regions. As the United States has produced more energy resources, particularly natural gas, trade flows and international markets have begun to adapt. The liquefied natural gas (LNG) that the United States expected to import is now available for others, and several LNG export terminals are currently under construction.[33]

Given these shifts, the United States has an opportunity to consider the foreign policy implications of increased natural gas supplies. Natural gas prices in the United States have been far below those in countries such as Japan or the United Kingdom, giving North America a considerable competitive edge in its energy costs.[34] Given the price differentials and potential for increased LNG exports, U.S. companies will have incentives and capacity to arbitrage and, in the process, reduce the large global differences in gas prices. *The Task Force believes U.S. natural gas exports could help dampen global market volatility, strengthen ties with U.S. allies, and offer geopolitical and diplomatic benefits. More open energy markets would also support U.S. aims for the international economy.*

NORTH AMERICA'S ENERGY POLICIES

Outdated government regulations and the absence of a regional framework hold back North American energy integration. Export and investment restrictions and varying regulatory approaches—heightened by domestic sensitivities—prevent the three nations from securing the economic and geopolitical gains generated by increasing output.

The U.S. president determines whether crude oil exports are in the national interest (exempting supplies sent to Canada for domestic consumption, which are minimal). U.S. oil exports would stimulate investment and raise oil production levels. Increased exports would reduce inefficiencies in North America's oil market, where many refineries are located far away from new production sites or are designed to process other types of crude.

U.S. natural gas exports—whether by pipeline or as liquefied natural gas—also require governmental approval. As of September 2014, the Department of Energy had granted thirty-seven permits for U.S. LNG exports to free trade partners and nine permits for exports to non–free trade partners.[35] The Federal Energy Regulatory Commission (FERC) has approved only three LNG export terminals—two based in Louisiana and a third in Texas. Another fourteen are pending approval.[36]

The construction of North America's energy infrastructure has delayed oil and gas development. With production often in remote locations, energy companies have been unable or unwilling to invest in the infrastructure necessary to move oil and gas from wells to refineries and then to consumers (Figures 7 and 8). North Dakota's Bakken formation, one of the United States' largest shale formations, continues to flare nearly one-third of its natural gas because of infrastructure limitations.[37] North America should build new pipelines and upgrade older ones, both within and among the three countries, to address the bottlenecks.

Without adequate pipeline capacity, energy companies have increasingly turned to the rails, roads, and waterways. The number of U.S. train cars filled with crude oil skyrocketed from around 9,300 in 2008 to 434,000 in 2013.[38] Between 2011 and 2012 alone, the numbers of trucks carrying crude to refineries increased by 38 percent and barges by 53 percent.[39] These alternative modes of transportation are expensive and raise safety concerns due to their greater likelihood of spills.[40]

Governments need to clarify rules to enable private financing to proceed. To construct or operate cross-border pipelines or other forms of energy infrastructure, developers must first obtain a presidential permit, for which the approval process can be long, laborious, and politically complicated. The reviewing government agency depends on the facility type—the U.S. Department of State oversees oil and oil product infrastructure requests, the Federal Energy Regulatory Commission

FIGURE 7: NORTH AMERICAN OIL PIPELINES

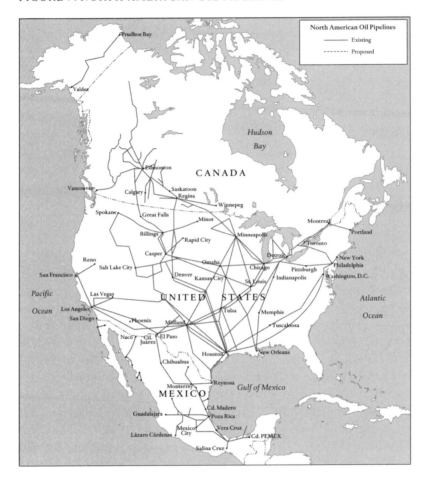

Sources: Canadian Energy Pipeline Association; Pemex; U.S. EIA; Canadian Association of Petroleum Producers.

reviews natural gas pipeline requests, and the U.S. Department of Energy oversees cross-border electricity projects.

The most well-known proposed North American energy infrastructure project is the Keystone XL pipeline, which would extend over two thousand miles to link the Canadian oil sands to the U.S. Gulf Coast refineries. Even though there are already seventy existing cross-border pipelines, and other ways to ship energy products from Canada's oil

FIGURE 8: NORTH AMERICAN GAS PIPELINES

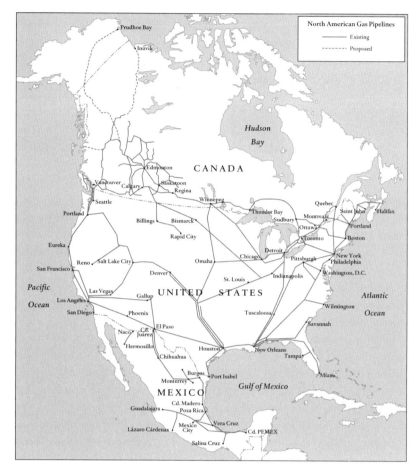

Sources: Canadian Energy Pipeline Association; Pemex; U.S. EIA.

sands to U.S. refineries, the U.S. government has repeatedly delayed the final decision on the pipeline. The delays have damaged U.S.-Canada relations and have the potential to slow, at the very least, greater North American energy integration. *The Task Force believes that U.S. energy infrastructure policies have failed to keep up with changing energy realities. This has limited the potential benefits to the broader U.S. economy and slowed North American energy integration.*

U.S. environmental policies also influence the pace and extent of energy exploration and production. Governments regulate oil and gas production on federal and state lands; federal onshore lands alone hold some 5.3 billion barrels of oil—nearly 20 percent of U.S. oil reserves.[41] U.S. laws such as the Clean Air Act, the Clean Water Act, and the Safe Drinking Water Act manage and set limits for U.S. water and air pollution and create standards for drinking water. Canada and Mexico have similar laws, which generally adhere to U.S. Environmental Protection Agency (EPA) and international community guidelines.

The three governments, as well as their civil societies, have a long history of working together on regional environmental issues, such as acid rain reduction and wildlife conservation. Nevertheless, North America lacks an effective, dedicated framework for discussing these issues, particularly as they pertain to the region's changing energy landscape. In 1994, NAFTA addressed cooperation on regional environmental regulations through a side agreement, but the Commission on Environmental Cooperation that was supposed to supervise these efforts has made little progress. The three governments created a new North American Energy Working Group in 2001 to address both environmental and energy production issues, but it was disbanded in 2009.

Without a trilateral framework, the region's energy sectors do not share best practices and lessons to the extent that they could. This interchange is particularly important given the rapid changes in energy technology and likelihood that mistakes or missteps will reverberate regionally. *The lack of tripartite institutions limits the potential for coordination regarding regulatory standards for smart grids, renewable energy incentives, technologies for lower carbon energy, barriers to trading energy products, energy efficiency guidelines, and other issues that have substantial implications for each country and for the region's energy integration.*

North America is undergoing an energy transformation. Regional cooperation and integration could boost the economic, geopolitical, and environmental benefits. If developed responsibly and sustainably, North America's energy boom could bring widespread gains to the three countries and their consumers, communities, and companies.

North American Economic Competitiveness

The Task Force believes that the United States' ability to compete in a dynamic and competitive world economy would be strengthened by enhanced economic ties with Canada and Mexico.

Globalization and regionalization have advanced together. Over the past two decades, North America's economic ties have deepened dramatically by almost all measures; they have the potential to develop even further. The region's trade grew from less than $300 billion in 1993 to more than $1.1 trillion in 2013 (Figure 9). The United States, Canada, and Mexico are among the most important trading partners for each other.[42]

Canada and Mexico are far more important to the U.S. economy than many U.S. citizens realize. The United States exports nearly five times as much to Mexico and Canada as it does to China and almost twice as much as to the European Union.[43] Mexico and Canada sell more than 75 percent of their exports within North America.[44]

FIGURE 9: NORTH AMERICAN TRADE

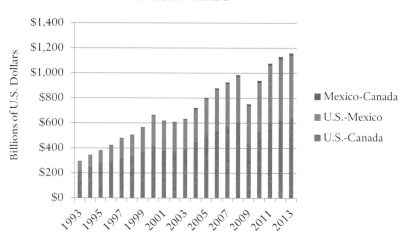

Sources: U.S. Census Bureau, Foreign Trade; Secretaría de la Economía, Mexico.

In 2011, approximately 150,000 U.S. companies sent goods—total-
ing a third of U.S. exports—to Mexico and Canada. These exchanges
extend far beyond the border states: Canada or Mexico is the top export
destination for forty-one of the fifty U.S. states (Figure 10). The export-
ing companies include not just well-known corporations such as General Motors, General Electric, and Procter & Gamble, but also more
than one hundred thousand small- and medium-size businesses.[45] A
recent Peterson Institute for International Economics report estimates
that U.S. exports to Canada and Mexico supported 2.6 million and 1.9
million U.S. jobs, respectively.[46]

The type of trade in North America has also changed—shifting from
primarily finished goods to pieces and parts that move back and forth
across borders as part of regional supply chains. A study by the National
Bureau of Economic Research reported that on average 40 percent of
the value of products imported from Mexico and 25 percent of those
from Canada actually come from the United States; the comparable
input percentage with the rest of the world is about 4 percent.[48] This

FIGURE 10: TOP EXPORT DESTINATION BY STATE[47]

Source: U.S. Census Bureau, Foreign Trade, 2013.

means that of the $280 billion in goods that the United States imported
from Mexico in 2013, some $112 billion of the value was created in the
United States; for the $322 billion that the United States imported from
Canada, the value created in the United States was $83 billion. Less
than $20 billion of the value from the $440 billion of U.S. imports from
China came from U.S. workers.[49]

The North American automotive industry is one of the most integrated sectors; roughly three out of every four export dollars remain
within the region.[50] The degree of interconnected production is also
impressive: automobiles often cross North America's borders several
times before completion. Other sectors are also deeply intertwined:
81 percent of the region's personal and household goods exports were
absorbed back into North America in 2012, along with 73 percent of iron
and steel and 72 percent of clothing (Figure 11).[51] In total, intra-regional
exports were 48 percent of North America's total exports in 2012.[52]

These high percentages reflect the shift toward continent-wide production over the past two decades. This integration has become important for the region's overall competitiveness and for employment in all
three nations.

Service industries have also become increasingly integrated,
spurred by investments and exchanges in areas such as banking, energy
services, express delivery, information technology, insurance, and

FIGURE 11: NORTH AMERICAN EXPORT DESTINATIONS

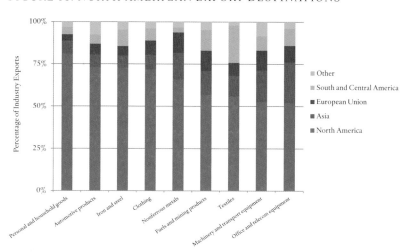

Source: World Trade Organization.

telecommunications. The regional trade in services has risen by nearly 200 percent—to well over $100 billion a year—despite licensing, visa, and other regulatory barriers.[53] There remain notable opportunities to integrate further in transportation, health care, money transfers, and energy.

Intra-regional cross-border investment has risen fourfold since 1993 to total an investment stock of some $780 billion by 2012.[54] More than 60 percent of this capital flowed from the United States to its neighbors. Yet Mexican and Canadian investments in the United States have also grown—particularly in the manufacturing, insurance, banking, and consumer sectors—reaching nearly $240 billion by 2012.[55] Mexican companies now own iconic brands such as Entenmann's, Sara Lee, Thomas' English Muffins, Weight Watchers, Mission Foods, and Trac-Fone cell phones, and Canadian products such as Lululemon Athletica gear, Bombardier planes, and BlackBerry devices have all become fixtures in American society.

The trade of goods and services, substantial foreign investment, and significant knowledge flows have enabled the United States, Canada, and Mexico to become more efficient and competitive together (Figure 12). Unfortunately, over the past decade, these movements have slowed, stagnated, and in some areas even receded.

In the years immediately following the Canada-United States Free Trade Agreement (CUSFTA), and then after the passage of NAFTA,

FIGURE 12: NORTH AMERICAN FOREIGN DIRECT INVESTMENT POSITIONS (1990–2012)

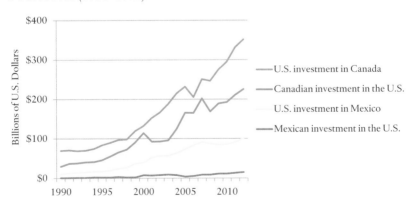

Source: OECD Database.

trade soared among the three nations, growing by more than 17 percent a year through 2000. Intra-regional exports reached a high point of 56 percent of North America's total exports in 2000—far greater than the 22 percent of intra-regional exports among Association of Southeast Asian Nation (ASEAN) countries and gaining on the 68 percent share within the European Union. However, since 2001 the annual rate of expansion in North American trade declined to an average of 6 percent, trailing the growth in North America's trade with the rest of the world.[56]

There are many reasons for the slowdown in North American economic integration. Major global trends and events—such as two economic recessions, China's entrance into the WTO in 2001, and Canada's and Mexico's efforts to diversify their trading partners—account for some of the slower pace. But U.S. policies also applied the brakes to North American integration, including NAFTA's limitations, inefficiencies along the border, and increased security costs after September 11, 2001.

U.S. POLICY

The 1994 North American Free Trade Agreement constructed the legal architecture undergirding North America as an economic zone. The agreement encouraged, formalized, and quickened a continental integration process that was already under way. NAFTA removed tariffs—some immediately and others gradually—for almost all goods, encouraged investment, and created common rules for issues such as intellectual property, transportation, and agricultural trade. NAFTA also was accompanied by labor and environmental side agreements, which were unprecedented at the time. Since 2001, similar provisions have been included within all U.S. free trade agreements.

Over the course of twenty years, NAFTA succeeded spectacularly in increasing trade and cross-border investment among the three countries. It also played a crucial role in transforming the way that companies produce their goods and spurred the creation of regional supply chains. By establishing the framework for a regional approach to global competitiveness, NAFTA laid the foundation for a stronger North America. It also provided a base for deeper economic cooperation and financial support for Mexico during its 1995 financial crisis, easing the extent of the downturn and enabling the relatively rapid economic rebound that followed.

Along with other free trade agreements, NAFTA helped increase consumer purchasing power, by both lowering prices and expanding options. A recent study by the Peterson Institute for International Economics estimates that U.S. households gained about one thousand dollars a year from NAFTA.[57]

In terms of jobs, the dreaded "giant sucking sound" of lost employment that Ross Perot predicted in 1992 never materialized. Instead, the rough consensus among scholars is that, in the years following NAFTA's start, the number of net new U.S. positions related to the free trade agreement ranged from zero to just under one million.[58]

Supporters of NAFTA also believe that it assisted Mexico as the country moved from a one-party corporatist state to a competitive democracy. NAFTA helped connect the institutions of Mexico to the North American political culture.

NAFTA nevertheless remains controversial in the United States. More than half of the Americans surveyed in a 2008 Gallup poll believed that NAFTA's economic effects have been mostly negative, compared to 23 percent of Mexicans and 39 percent of Canadians who hold the same view.[59] A 2008 Chicago Council on Global Affairs survey revealed that 64 percent of Americans believed that NAFTA threatened U.S. workers' job security and 55 percent believed it was detrimental to the U.S. economy.[60] However, attitudes about trade and North American economic integration vary considerably depending on how the question is phrased.[61]

Negative perceptions of NAFTA within the United States may be due in part to the uneven distribution of benefits from trade. As with any free trade agreement, there are winners and losers, and the increased regional integration following NAFTA led to changes that benefited the country as a whole but not all individuals or sectors. Some industries expanded while others contracted, and, as a result, some factories closed, even as others opened. For most workers, the shifts had insignificant or even positive effects on their income levels, but the transition was more difficult for pockets of U.S. workers in low-skilled manufacturing positions.[62] Although job losses related to factories shutting down and moving abroad were estimated at only about 2 percent of total losses, the narrative of these losses has had an outsize influence on shaping the NAFTA discussion within the United States.[63] In Mexico, meanwhile, the critiques have centered on the effects on rural subsistence farmers as NAFTA accelerated the economic transition from agriculture to manufacturing and services, although these negative assumptions also do not stand up to analysis.[64]

Other NAFTA criticisms center on the still-large economic disparities among the three trading partners (e.g., the lack of economic convergence), the agreement's limited effects on unauthorized immigration flows, and the frequent differences between environmental rules and on-the-ground practices. NAFTA, as a trade and investment agreement, was never likely to resolve these larger trilateral issues. There are also extensive debates among economists about the relative weights of trade, shifts in technology, productivity, educational attainment, and the role of unions, among other factors, in causing economic change.

Some also believe that public attitudes about NAFTA have been biased by the absence of governmental and other responses to the critiques. It is hard to win an argument if only one side makes its case. In recent years, the U.S. administration has sought to avoid even referring to NAFTA.

There is now a need for a twenty-first-century upgrade in the economic relationship among the three countries to address issues that were not included in NAFTA. NAFTA did not adequately address energy and the movement of people. Over the past two decades, new issues have arisen or been transformed—such as e-commerce and digital trade, cybersecurity, intellectual property, mutual recognition of standards and regulatory coherence, and a host of environmental topics.

The Task Force strongly believes that NAFTA has been of significant net benefit for the continent. By expanding regional trade in goods and services, boosting cross-border investment, deepening the integration of production processes, maintaining and creating jobs, lowering prices, and creating higher-quality goods, it has benefited North American businesses, workers, and consumers. NAFTA also boosted societal and governmental ties at a time of sweeping political change in Mexico. In light of global changes of the past twenty years, however, NAFTA alone cannot meet the needs and opportunities of North American integration.

TODAY'S BARRIERS TO TRADE

In the process of reducing economic barriers, NAFTA exposed and even created other limitations to regional trade and economic integration. NAFTA's rules-of-origin provisions have proved cumbersome. The three countries developed these provisions to ensure that the FTA's preferential tariff treatment applied only to products made within the free-trade zone. Different goods require varying percentages of components to be made within the NAFTA countries; for example, 62.5 percent of cars, light trucks, engines, and transmissions must be produced within North America in order to qualify for duty-free treatment.[65] To prove that products meet the rules of origin, firms must complete certificates of origin. Given the administrative costs, some eligible firms simply opt to pay a tariff instead of submitting documentation. The cost to firms of compliance with the requirements is high—one estimate places it at around $35 billion a year—undermining the purpose of NAFTA and the economic advantages it was intended to provide.[66]

Other customs paperwork also burdens North American companies. Although electronic documents are becoming more common for U.S. agencies, there is not one unified portal for submissions or information sharing among the forty-seven U.S. agencies that deal directly with the existing import/export process. These offices range from the Animal and Plant Health Inspection Service and the U.S. Census Bureau to the Office of the U.S. Trade Representative and the Food and Drug Administration (FDA).[67] President Barack Obama signed an executive order—in the context of the February 2014 North American Leaders' Summit—mandating the completion of a U.S. electronic "single window" customs system by December 2016, but the U.S. government has struggled to implement other such policy directives.[68] This initiative should be tracked carefully to ensure execution.

Regulatory differences pose another significant barrier. It is understandable that each country has rules to ensure that food products are safe, ecosystems are protected, and labor standards are met; nevertheless, the differences among these laws create costs for companies and consumers and raise the question of whether North American commonalities or mutual recognition is possible. Some regulations are vastly different, but others, such as label sizes, seem to incorporate trivial variances.[69] The incongruent regulations require multiple tests and certifications for the same goods. For example, crash tests for new vehicles can cost anywhere from $120,000 to $150,000 per test. If a car is exported, it is likely that the test will have to be repeated—raising production costs without ensuring greater safety.[70] The administration of regulations by U.S. Customs and Border Protection (CBP) officials also adds to the inspection time for commercial shipments.

In an effort to address these regulatory issues, the United States created two separate initiatives: the High-Level Regulatory Cooperation
Council with Mexico (HLRCC) in 2010 and the U.S.-Canada Regulatory Cooperation Council (RCC) in 2011. The U.S.-Mexico Council
focuses on seven sectoral issues—ranging from food safety to nano-
technology—while the U.S.-Canada Council encompasses twenty-
nine specific initiatives, including motor vehicle safety, train emissions,
and meat and poultry export certifications.[71] Though the two groups
have made some important gains, progress has been slow and the scope
of these initiatives is limited.

The United States has also taken unilateral steps that have slowed
and even reversed the gains from integration. One example is the country of origin labeling (COOL) rules for meat. In 2002, the United States
began requiring certain meat products to list the animal's country of
origin. This requirement is protectionism in the guise of labeling. In
2013, the United States expanded these protectionist rules, requiring
meat labels to list not only the country where the animal was born, but
also where it was raised and slaughtered. The new regulations also mandate that animals from different countries be kept apart, discouraging
imports of calves and hogs and disrupting the highly integrated North
American market for bearing, raising, feeding, transporting, and pro-
cessing animals. Canada and Mexico have brought a complaint to the
World Trade Organization (they won their original complaint against
the COOL rules in 2012); if the United States loses and does not comply,
the two neighbors will then be able to raise barriers to U.S. products,
further closing North American markets instead of opening them.

BORDER-CROSSING WOES

The United States has failed to fulfill its NAFTA obligation to open
its roads and permit safe cross-border services. Mexican trucks were
supposed to be able to operate in four U.S. states—Texas, California,
New Mexico, and Arizona—by December 1995 and then throughout
the continental United States by January 1, 2000.[72] Almost fifteen years
later, the vast majority of Mexican trucks still are not allowed on U.S.
roads. Mexico has retaliated in kind, blocking the movement of U.S.
trucks within its borders. It has also introduced retaliatory tariffs to be
applied on a yearly rotating basis to a variety of U.S. imports.[73]

The rationalization for the delay, offered by labor unions in particular, has been safety. To meet the alleged concerns, the U.S. government developed pilot programs, which have consistently demonstrated that participating Mexican drivers and trucks had equal or better safety records than their U.S. counterparts.[74] Despite the evidence, opponents of competition in trucking services have blocked the opening. The most recent effort, begun in 2011, includes only forty-five trucks, a meager number compared to the fourteen thousand that cross the border from Mexico daily.

The U.S. failure to live up to NAFTA's rules is costly in terms of money, time, fuel, and pollution for the United States and Mexico. A Mexican truck must unload its goods at a warehouse on the Mexican side of the border to be picked up by a short-haul truck. This truck moves the goods to another warehouse on the U.S. side, where they are packed onto a third truck for delivery to their final destination.[75] By the same token, U.S. exporters are forced to incur drayage costs to transport truck trailers across the border and find Mexican partners to deliver the goods to their final destination. The added time and costs suppress trade.

Physical barriers also delay transit and hinder economic competitiveness. Heightened inspection measures (which are discussed in detail in the next section) slow crossings at U.S. ports of entry. As the volume of people, cars, trucks, and goods escalated over the past decades, chronic underinvestment in border infrastructure has slowed the movement of goods and trade. Today, the average age of U.S. ports of entry is forty years, with many closer to seventy years old.[76] Few new crossings have been opened and even basic maintenance on existing infrastructure has been deferred, at times to a dangerous degree. The combination of escalating demand with ailing border infrastructure has created a burdensome trade and travel environment that is difficult to police, producing significant backlogs and stress for inspection authorities.

Reports by the U.S. Government Accountability Office (GAO) and the Woodrow Wilson Mexico Institute highlight regional studies that measure border transit delays: the waits routinely exceed an hour or longer at heavily congested commercial ports, such as those between San Diego and Tijuana, and Laredo and Nuevo Laredo.[77] These studies consistently show that such long wait times elevate costs for companies, workers, and border cities.

Away from the immediate border, transportation and other infrastructure investment within the NAFTA countries has also lagged. The

American Society of Civil Engineers gave the United States a "D+" for the quality of its infrastructure, estimating the need for $3.6 trillion in investment by 2020 to fill the cumulative deficit.[78] According to a World Economic Forum report, nearly 10 percent of U.S. business respondents to questions on trade facilitation identified "high cost or delays caused by domestic transportation" as the most problematic factor for exporting goods.[79] The World Economic Forum's *Global Competitiveness Report 2013–2014* ranks the United States nineteenth out of 148 countries in the quality of its infrastructure; Canada is slightly ahead at sixteenth, while Mexico ranks sixty-sixth.[80] *The Task Force finds that underinvestment in North American infrastructure adds significant costs to each country and hurts regional competitiveness.*

Several infrastructure bills have been introduced in the U.S. Congress in recent years, including the Partnership to Build America Act of 2014 and the Building and Renewing Infrastructure for Development and Growth in Employment (BRIDGE) Act, but none has been able to garner sufficient support to become law. State and local governments have made more progress, with more than thirty U.S. states enacting laws that enable public-private partnerships (PPPs), encouraging more private-sector infrastructure financing. The diversity and complexity of these agreements and local officials' uneven expertise limit their usefulness.

There are few dedicated financing mechanisms to fill the infrastructure gap in the border region. The North American Development Bank (NADB), created through NAFTA, has authorized capital of just $3 billion, and its mandate extends only to environmental or health projects.

STEPS TOWARD BETTER BORDER MANAGEMENT

In an effort to expedite commercial transit and improve security at the border (the latter discussed in detail in the next section), the U.S. government has launched several programs. These initiatives include the Customs-Trade Partnership Against Terrorism (C-TPAT), through which U.S. Customs and Border Protection works with registered companies to enhance security along supply chains. C-TPAT members are eligible for Free and Secure Trade (FAST) lanes at ports of entry along the U.S.-Canadian and U.S.-Mexican borders. Yet some participants complain that the program has neither reduced the number of truck inspections nor significantly speeded transit times.

The United States launched the Beyond the Border program with Canada in 2011. The program's economic goals include upgrading infrastructure, streamlining customs procedures, measuring border wait times more accurately, and harmonizing shipment processes. It also seeks to expand trusted-traveler and preclearance programs, strengthen governmental collaboration with the private sector, and broaden U.S.-Canadian security cooperation beyond the physical border. The U.S.-Mexico Twenty-First Century Border Management initiative, though less expansive in scope, seeks to achieve similar and in some instances identical objectives to those with Canada. *The Task Force recognizes significant advances in border management, particularly along the U.S.-Canadian border, and believes these efforts should continue and, where possible, be expanded trilaterally.*

A new U.S.-Mexico High-Level Economic Dialogue brings together members of the U.S. Departments of Commerce and State, the Office of the U.S. Trade Representative, and their Mexican counterparts to advance bilateral trade and competitiveness. U.S. vice president Joseph R. Biden Jr. led the first meeting in Mexico in September 2013, alongside Mexican finance secretary Luis Videgaray and Mexican foreign secretary José Antonio Meade.

BEYOND NAFTA: NEW CROSS-REGIONAL ECONOMIC AND TRADE AGREEMENTS

The most potentially transformative discussions for North America's economies today could be the negotiations for the Trans-Pacific Partnership and the Transatlantic Trade and Investment Partnership. The TPP aims to create an integrated economic platform that spans the Pacific Ocean, bringing together the NAFTA partners along with Australia, Japan, Malaysia, Peru, Vietnam, Brunei Darussalam, Chile, New Zealand, and Singapore and representing a combined GDP of $27 trillion.[81] The United States already has FTAs with six of the other eleven countries involved. The United States was slow in supporting the addition of Canada and Mexico to the TPP negotiations, thereby underappreciating the role and integration of the North American market. In addition to expanding trade and investment across the Pacific, the TPP offers an opportunity to modernize and upgrade rules for all the participants—including in North America. *The Task Force believes that the TPP provides an important opportunity to build on NAFTA's gains, consider common North American interests, and move beyond limitations of the twenty-year-old NAFTA framework.*

The TTIP negotiations between the United States and the European Union do not include Mexico and Canada. Mexico signed an FTA with the European Union in 2000, and Canada completed its own negotiations in 2013. *The Task Force believes that the unwillingness of the United States to include its North American partners at the TTIP table is short-sighted and conflicts with the goal of building a more competitive North American market.* Although more participants can add to negotiating complexity, it is important for the United States to gain Canadian and Mexican perspectives about the effects of TTIP provisions on their economies. The North American auto industry, for example, is deeply integrated, so TTIP rules would affect the Canadian parts and Mexican assembly industries. Separate agreements with the EU are likely to lead to costly rules of origin and additional costs.

The administration will need trade promotion authority (TPA) to complete and pass the TPP and TTIP. TPA enables the executive branch to present trade agreements to the Congress for an up-or-down vote without amendment. Congress' last grant of TPA expired in 2007. *Without TPA, the Task Force believes North America will not be able to update its trade rules for the twenty-first century.*

Over the past twenty years, the three North American economies have become much more deeply integrated—through cross-border trade, the joint production of goods, and foreign investment. However, a host of barriers limit further integration and even endanger the gains that have been made. The North American governments should increase their global economic competitiveness by building on NAFTA through closer regional cooperation connected to current and future challenges.

North American Security

North America has come a long way from its nineteenth-century wars to today's peaceful cooperation. The continent enjoys the longest peaceful borders in the world. Together, the three partners now confront common threats—terrorism, crime, natural disasters, health epidemics, cybersecurity, and drug trafficking. They face the task of making passage efficient and seamless for lawful travelers and trade while stopping criminals and countering dangers. The United States has increasingly viewed its borders as a source of vulnerability, underappreciating the strength that could come from a much closer and more coordinated regional approach to protecting North America's peoples.

For many years, unauthorized immigration was the United States' predominant border concern. These worries increased during the 1980s and 1990s as migration grew. Migrant apprehensions along the United States' southwest border peaked in 2001 at 1.6 million.[82]

In the wake of September 11, terrorism jumped to the top of North America's security priorities. Though none of the terrorists came into the United States through border crossings, the assault exposed the United States' vulnerability to attacks on its soil; border security became the locus of new efforts to keep the nation safe. The threat posed by international terrorist organizations, largely based outside North America, continues to reverberate across the continent.

The proliferation of transnational criminal organizations operating along the southern U.S. border and beyond is another twenty-first-century threat. Often dubbed "drug cartels," Mexico-based entities dominate the Western Hemisphere's narcotics trade, exploiting their comparative geographic advantage next to the world's largest consumer of illegal substances: the United States. These groups do not limit themselves to smuggling illicit narcotics; they also extort, kidnap, steal, and traffic all types of contraband and people. Mexico continues to struggle to develop the institutions and capabilities to defend its democratic rule of law. U.S. concerns have grown with the violence.

Estimates vary, but Mexico's insecurity appears to shave at least a percentage point off Mexico's GDP each year.[83] Given North America's commercial integration, these costs spill over to the country's neighbors. The violence weakens the robustness of regional supply chains as some businesses decide to locate production elsewhere, thereby impeding the virtuous cycle of investment, production, employment, and consumer demand.

Heavy security at the border can slow trade and hurt economies and livelihoods throughout the region. It can also make the ports of entry more chaotic as companies seek to bypass stricter security measures through informal workarounds. The disorder actually reduces security, making it more difficult for the CBP and other agencies to do their jobs. *The Task Force believes border security and efficiency need not be a zero-sum game. The right policies can both speed the flow of legal goods and people and intercept illegal and dangerous ones.*

U.S. POLICY

The principal U.S. response to undocumented immigration, terrorism, and transnational criminal groups has been to provide more resources for patrolling the borders. In the past decade, the number of Border Patrol agents on the United States' southwest border has more than doubled—from 8,580 in 2000 to 18,611 in 2013—and those on the northern border increased from 306 to 2,156.[84] The Border Patrol's budget has risen by more than 200 percent to reach some $3.4 billion in 2013.[85] Adding in Immigration and Customs Enforcement (ICE) and other immigration enforcement programs, total funding reached more than $18 billion in fiscal year (FY) 2014—more than all other major federal law enforcement agencies combined.

To address undocumented immigration throughout the 1990s, the U.S. government conducted targeted campaigns to reduce illegal crossings in specific densely populated areas. These programs—including Operation Hold the Line in El Paso, Operation Gatekeeper in San Diego, and Operation Safeguard in Phoenix—increased the number of agents, border resources, and fencing in those areas.

These local models subsequently became institutionalized along the entire border. The 2006 Secure Fence Act mandated fencing along "not less than 700 miles" of the southwest border.[86] For the other nearly 1,300 miles, legislation ordered a combination of intelligence and biometric screening, including remote surveillance equipment, underground sensors, and even unarmed predator drones. U.S. law enforcement also conducted a number of operations away from the border, including workplace raids and audits. However, the United States' overarching policy toward unauthorized immigration remains concentrated at the border.

The devastation of September 11, 2001, catapulted global terrorism to the forefront of policymakers' agendas. To address this danger, the United States reached out separately to each North American neighbor, creating bilateral—instead of trilateral—security agreements. With Canada, this resulted in the Smart Border Declaration and Action Plan, which encompassed intelligence sharing, cargo screening, and border management. With Mexico, the new security arrangement took the form of the U.S.-Mexico Border Partnership Agreement— also known as the Smart Border Accord—which focused on a similar, though more limited, set of issues as well as border infrastructure. Both agreements included biometrics and prescreening programs (such as NEXUS at the U.S.-Canadian border and the Secure Electronic Network for Travelers Rapid Inspection, or SENTRI, at the U.S.-Mexican border) and created common standards for assessing individual and commercial vehicle risk levels.

A renewed interest in tracking who was entering and leaving the United States resulted in a push to record all arrivals and exits. A tracking system had been mandated in the 1996 Immigration Act but was never implemented.[87] After the September 11 attacks, the U.S. government began collecting biometric records on entries through the United States Visitor and Immigrant Status Indicator Technology (US-VISIT) program; the U.S. government initially collected this information at airports and later did so for third-country nationals crossing land borders. More recently, the United States began tracking airport departures and exchanging data with Canada on entries and exits. These efforts were combined with monitoring databases such as the Automated Biometric Identification System (IDENT), which rapidly compares fingerprints against a national criminal database. In 2007, the Western Hemisphere

Travel Initiative required all North American citizens to carry a passport or passport card when crossing U.S. borders, ending the earlier, more lenient identification policies. However, the United States has still not created a comprehensive entry-exit system.

The September 11 attacks also led to the creation of the U.S. Department of Homeland Security (DHS), merging many agencies and responsibilities. Border control—through CBP, ICE, and U.S. Citizenship and Immigration Services (USCIS)—represents the largest portion of DHS' budget, reinforcing a border-centric approach to preventing terrorism and undocumented immigration.

President George W. Bush also established the United States Northern Command (NORTHCOM) in 2002. NORTHCOM expanded the U.S. military's role in defending North America from terrorism and other national security threats. The new command's area of responsibility encompasses the land, sea, and air from the Arctic down to Mexico's southern border. NORTHCOM works closely with U.S. civilian agencies—the Department of Homeland Security, Federal Bureau of Investigation, Central Intelligence Agency, National Security Agency, and Federal Emergency Management Agency, among others. NORTHCOM also coordinates closely with both Canadian and Mexican military and security agencies; it is linked to NORAD, the U.S.-Canada air defense partnership that dates back to the 1950s, through a shared commander.

To help address rising violence and organized crime, the United States expanded bilateral security cooperation and aid to Mexico through the 2008 Mérida Initiative, which promised $1.4 billion over three years to support Mexico's law enforcement.[88] This undertaking represented a fundamental shift in bilateral relations, overcoming Mexico's historical resistance to involvement with the U.S. military and security services. The Obama administration revised and expanded the Mérida Initiative's mission in 2010, shifting from an emphasis on military equipment to a comprehensive bilateral strategy that seeks to reduce the operations and influence of organized crime. The initiative now encompasses the following four pillars: disrupting the operational capacity of organized crime; institutionalizing the rule of law; creating a twenty-first-century border; and building strong and resilient communities.

POLICY CONSEQUENCES: INTENDED
AND UNINTENDED

U.S. policies have added security but have also slowed the movement of legitimate people and goods. The number of personal vehicles crossing the border through U.S. ports of entry fell over the past decade from 129 million cars in 2000 to 95 million in 2012, and total passengers dropped from 329 million to 177 million.[89] The number of bus and train passengers and pedestrians also fell, reflecting the growing wait times, security checks, and difficulties of making border crossings.[90] Stricter inspections and the longer wait times make trade more expensive. These constraints damage the binational fluidity that has defined border communities for decades, changing the traditional way of life for residents who live along the border.

Programs such as SENTRI, NEXUS, Global Entry, C-TPAT, and FAST have reduced wait times by separating trusted and lesser-known travelers. The U.S.-Canada Beyond the Border initiative includes modest joint law enforcement activities such as Operation Shiprider, which teams U.S. Coast Guard and Royal Canadian Mounted Police officers to patrol shared waterways. U.S. federal law enforcement officials have forged Integrated Border Enforcement Teams with their Canadian counterparts to share information on cross-border law enforcement issues. The United States and Mexico have launched the Twenty-First Century Border Management initiative.

New pilot programs are designed to overcome some problems while meeting security standards. In June 2013, the United States and Canada launched a pre-inspection initiative at the Pacific Highway border crossing south of Vancouver and at the Buffalo and Fort Erie Peace Bridge; this pilot places U.S. Customs and Border Protection officers on the Canadian side of the border to clear U.S.-bound goods before they reach the physical border. Mexico's customs office is pre-clearing air cargo bound from Laredo, Texas, to Mexico. CBP officers will soon be pre-clearing goods in Mexico for entry at Otay Mesa, San Diego. Both countries are discussing a similar project along the U.S.-Mexico border outside El Paso, Texas.

The Task Force finds that, over a decade after the shock of September 11, U.S. border management efforts have not maximized security at the lowest reasonable cost. As a result, North American integration has been harmed—creating unnecessary losses for all three countries. New pilots and initiatives hold promise, but they should be tested and, where appropriate, expanded. The U.S. government and its Canadian and Mexican partners should pursue a process of continuous border innovation.

The Mérida Initiative against drug trafficking and organized crime has had uneven results. Since 2009, Mexico has successfully captured or killed more than two-thirds of the most-wanted drug traffickers and substantially disrupted the operations of powerful criminal networks.[91] Many of these high-profile operations resulted from bilateral intelligence and cooperation. Yet the removal of top drug traffickers has led quickly to successors, or consolidation with other cartels. Targeting "kingpins" should be part of a larger strategy of atomization, dismantling large criminal organizations by fragmenting them into many smaller groups that can then be effectively countered by professionalized police and a functioning criminal justice system.

The fight against crime and violence requires an effective domestic judicial system. Mexico has strengthened the rule of law, but many challenges remain. Mexico's law enforcement and supreme court have substantially increased their independence and professionalism over the past three decades. A set of constitutional and legislative reforms in 2008 set in motion a fundamental transformation of the court system, though the implementation of these changes has been slow. Even as Mexico nears the 2016 deadline for the transition to the new system, only about half of its thirty-one states have fully overhauled their judicial structures.[92] In the meantime, Mexico has used extradition to try many of its most lethal criminals in U.S. courts.

Mexico has expanded and professionalized its federal police, although it remains just 10 percent of Mexico's police forces, even with the addition of a new five-thousand-person gendarmerie. State and local police, comprising some 350,000 officers, often remain underfunded, underpaid, and unreliable.

Initiatives to modernize the border and build "resilient communities"—the third and fourth pillars of the Mérida Initiative—lag even farther behind. Investment in ports of entry and border infrastructure has not matched the increase in trade. Furthermore, programs to address the underlying socioeconomic factors behind rising crime rates are limited to a few pilots in cities such as Ciudad Juárez.

U.S. aid flows to Mexico have increased from around $70 million in 2005—before the Mérida Initiative—to roughly $250 million a year from FY2011 to FY2014. (The FY2015 expenditure is expected to fall to $130 million).[93] This spending is small compared to U.S. outlays in Afghanistan—which receives more than $2 billion per year—or in the context of Mexico's annual federal security budget of some $11 billion in FY2014.[94] Canada sent $13 million in foreign aid to Mexico in 2012.[95]

Finally, despite emphasizing shared responsibility for much of Mexico's violence, the United States has done little to address domestic factors that affect Mexico's security. Illegal flows of weapons continue unabated. The Bureau of Alcohol, Tobacco, Firearms, and Explosives (ATF) traced 70 percent of a sample of seized guns provided by Mexican authorities between 2008 and 2012 to dealers in the United States.[96] The expiration of the Federal Assault Weapons Ban in 2004 lifted the prohibition on the manufacture of certain types of semiautomatic firearms for civilian use. Some research has shown its absence has made it easier to obtain assault weapons in Mexico, in particular close to the U.S.-Mexico border.[97]

An estimated $6 billion to $29 billion a year in illegal Mexican drug revenues enters into licit financial systems through banks, business, and trade-based money laundering.[98] U.S. illegal drug consumption continues to pull drugs northward (even as the United States produces a significant amount of its own drugs). And while the consumption of cocaine and methamphetamine has fallen, the use of other drugs—particularly marijuana, opioid pain relievers, and the black tar heroin produced in Mexico—has grown.[99] The 2012 National Survey on Drug Use and Health finds that overall roughly 9 percent, or 28 million people, in the United States over the age of twelve had used illegal drugs in the past month.[100]

The Task Force believes that the United States and Canada have a shared interest and responsibility with Mexico in combating drug trafficking and organized crime and in strengthening Mexico's democratic rule of law. These regional threats require regional responses.

THINKING CONTINENTALLY

Close ties among the three countries' law enforcement agencies have led to a number of successful security efforts, especially in identifying and keeping suspected criminals or terrorists out of the region. Nevertheless, the U.S. focus on border control can be counterproductive, displacing rather than reducing risk. *The Task Force believes that the United States should shift from border-centric security toward a strategy of combining perimeter protection with security in depth through the use of intelligence, risk assessment, shared capabilities, and joint actions throughout the region.*

Almost all of the United States' current regional security efforts have been based on dual bilateralism: the United States creates two separate and parallel sets of policies for Mexico and Canada. Although the U.S.-Canada Beyond the Border framework takes steps toward continental security, it leaves Mexico out. Likewise, the U.S.-Mexico Twenty-First Century Border Management initiative excludes Canada.

This dual bilateralism divides North America. It discourages even discussing—much less promoting—a trilateral approach to security. Bilateral security efforts can often make it easier to solve problems and develop border management models. However, by emphasizing the differences between the U.S.-Canadian and the U.S.-Mexican security relationships, rather than the commonalities, the United States forgoes advantages of a continental approach. For example, regional intelligence sharing and threat detection could help mitigate threats before they ever reach U.S. borders. *The Task Force acknowledges the differences between the U.S.-Mexican and U.S.-Canadian security relationships but believes that the development of a comprehensive North American security approach, over time, would improve U.S. and North American security.*

EMERGING THREATS

By encouraging a North American perspective, the United States can also promote combined assessments of and actions on broader security challenges. Organized crime in Central America is a serious security issue for North America. Located between the Andean cocaine producers and Mexico's drug transit corridors, Central America's countries face severe threats from the Western Hemisphere's drug trafficking. Consider homicide rates of 90 per 100,000 people in Honduras, 44 per 100,000 in Belize, 41 per 100,000 in El Salvador, and 40 per 100,000 in Guatemala—compared to 30 per 100,000 in Colombia and 31 per 100,000 in South Africa. Central America is one of the world's most violent regions, with entrenched criminal gangs and threatened political and governmental institutions.[101] The recent surge of children fleeing Central America underscores the direct effects of these dangers on the United States.

The Central American-Dominican Republic Free Trade Agreement (CAFTA-DR) offers economic possibilities for these small countries, but growth, investment, and economic opportunity require security, effective governance, and safety. Drug traffickers and gangs have corrupted fragile institutions. North America faces a risk of threatened states on its southern border. *To counter this danger, North America should combine security, good governance, rule of law, and economic opportunity—in a fashion analogous to Plan Colombia.* The Caribbean region also periodically poses risks of instability, drug trafficking, migration, and organized crime. *The Task Force believes that North America should address security challenges in Central America and the Caribbean more effectively and efficiently by working together.*

The Arctic—North America's fourth coast—poses new security challenges too. The Arctic is soon expected to resemble the Baltic Sea, with an ice layer during the winter but navigable by vessels at other times of the year. This dramatic change will present new economic opportunities and security issues—including new shipping channels, which may significantly cut travel times between Asia and Europe; new industrial fishing; and large hydrocarbon and mineral reserves.

Arctic governance requires coordination among many nations and interests. The Arctic Council—composed of the United States, Canada, Denmark, Finland, Iceland, Norway, Russia, and Sweden—offers a forum for designing a comprehensive framework for the region.

The United States has only one active heavy icebreaker, *Polar Star*, and one medium icebreaker, *Healy*, with plans to add a third ship. Canada has six icebreakers, though none heavy, and is planning the construction of one additional vessel. Russia maintains four active heavy icebreakers and six medium icebreakers.[102] *The ice is melting faster than the policies to govern the Arctic are being developed. The Task Force believes that North America would be best served by a unified planning and execution of Arctic policy.*

North American Community

The United States, Canada, and Mexico are increasingly linked through individuals, families, and communities. Some thirty-four million Mexicans and Mexican-Americans and more than three million Canadians and Canadian-Americans live in the United States. Nearly one million U.S. expatriates and a large number of Canadians live, at least part of the year, in Mexico. Another one million to two million U.S. citizens and a growing number of Mexicans live in Canada.

Shorter stays are numerous. U.S. citizens choose Mexico for their getaways more than any other foreign locale. Mexicans and Canadians return the favor, comprising the largest groups of tourists entering the United States: a combined thirty-four million visitors each year who contribute an estimated $35 billion to the U.S. economy.[103] Workers, students, and shoppers routinely cross the borders; there were 230 million land border crossings in 2012, or roughly 630,000 a day.[104] Indigenous communities also span the border, with residents frequently crossing back and forth.

North America also shares a workforce: companies and corporations now make products and provide services in all three countries. With integrated supply chains, employees in one country depend on the performance of those in another; together, they contribute to the quality and competitiveness of final products that are sold regionally or globally.

The North American community extends beyond people. The region shares the air, water, and biodiversity, as well as the challenges of natural disasters, pollution, and viruses. North America's leaders should both recognize and better manage these diverse and extensive continental connections.

IMMIGRATION

The CFR-sponsored Independent Task Force Report on U.S. Immigration Policy from 2009 delves into these complex and controversial subjects.[105] The movement of people across North America is a critical component of the continent's potential. The ability to build a stronger and more competitive North America will depend, in significant part, on the future regional labor force.

Over the past thirty years, an unprecedented wave of Mexicans traveled north to the United States. Many came in search of economic betterment. Demographics, too, played an important role in pushing many young Mexicans to immigrate to the United States. In the 1960s and 1970s, Mexico's mortality rate fell faster than the fertility rate, creating a youth bulge in the 1980s and 1990s that flooded the weak domestic job market. The U.S. economy—combined with weak border and workplace enforcement and limited immigration numbers for low-skilled workers—created a large demand for people.

Mexicans became the United States' largest immigrant group, comprising roughly a third of all migrants. Mexican immigrants peaked at more than twelve million in 2009—equal to some 10 percent of Mexico's total population.[106] In recent years, this movement has begun to recede.[107] Today, net migration between the United States and Mexico stands at zero. Indeed, Asians have recently supplanted Hispanics as the largest group of new immigrants arriving in the United States.[108] This decline in Mexican immigration results from changes in the factors that originally drew Mexicans to the United States: shifts in economic prospects, demographics, and opportunities at home.

Canada is even more dependent on migrants, with more than 20 percent of its population born in a different country. Few of these immigrants come from the United States or Mexico; the countries with the most migrants to Canada include the Philippines, India, and China. Canada has used an immigration "points system" that favors high-skilled immigrants and encourages more rapid integration by prioritizing those immigrants who have already spent time in Canada.

As a traditional country of emigration, Mexico's immigration policies are different from those of its northern neighbors. These dynamics are beginning to change. With roughly 1.4 million former emigrants returning to Mexico between 2005 and 2010, the country can utilize the skills and capital that migrants bring home. Mexico also now faces an inflow of people born abroad—immigrants grew from just under five hundred thousand in 2000 to almost one million in 2010. More than three-quarters of these immigrants were born in the United States; the vast majority are children under the age of fifteen.[109] Mexico is also an important transit country for hundreds of thousands of Central American immigrants en route to the United States.[110]

U.S. immigration and labor mobility policies lag the deepened economic and demographic ties between the three sovereign nations. *The Task Force believes that a stronger and more united North America needs coherent policies for the movement of people within the region—and that the laws that reflect these policies should be enforced.*

ECONOMIC GROWTH

Most economists believe that immigration is a net benefit for an economy, but that gains are unevenly distributed. Benefits vary by race, gender, and educational levels. Some early studies found that native-born men in the United States who lack a high school degree are set back by immigration, losing an estimated two dollars a week in earnings. Previous immigrants are also hurt as they compete with the new arrivals.[111] More recent estimates, however, do not find that immigration harms any educational or gender category, though they find that some categories benefit much more than others.[112] Studies suggest that much of the downward pressure on wages stems from the unauthorized status of illegal workers rather than from immigration. A Center for American Progress report estimated that providing a path to legalization would raise wages for undocumented workers by 15 percent.[113]

Immigrants can help revive struggling neighborhoods and increase consumer demand for goods and services. Immigrants open businesses and create jobs—in 2011, they started 28 percent of all new U.S. companies, employing one in ten U.S. workers.[114] Still, some communities receiving immigrants have struggled to include people from different backgrounds or cultures, even while benefiting economically.

Immigrants also pay taxes and use public services. A study by the National Research Council estimates that immigrants in the United States, including the undocumented, pay on average nearly $1,800 more in taxes than they receive in benefits.[115] The U.S. Congressional

Budget Office estimates that an immigration reform that changes the legal status of undocumented workers would have a net benefit for U.S. revenues, boosting federal income and social security tax inflows by some $450 billion over the next decade even as federal spending for these immigrants is expected to increase by $261 billion, primarily for tax credits and health care—adding up to a $197 billion surplus over the next ten years.[116]

The Task Force believes that the enforcement of immigration laws and the establishment of appropriate policy objectives are critical to maximizing the significant contributions immigrants make to North American communities, economic growth, and regional competitiveness.

U.S. POLICY

The focus of U.S. policy in recent years has been on undocumented immigration, with a priority of safeguarding the border and stopping flows of unauthorized people. Between 2009 and 2013, the Obama administration deported nearly two million individuals, with Mexicans making up the vast majority. Over the past two years, however, the removals have included increasing numbers of Central Americans.

Individual states have enacted a steady stream of immigration-related legislation, passing more than 1,900 laws and resolutions between 2008 and 2013.[117] Some of the initiatives were restrictive, punishing landlords or businesses that rent to or hire undocumented immigrants or making it a criminal offense for immigrants not to have official identification on hand. Yet sixty cities—including San Francisco, New York, Washington, Houston, and Philadelphia—designated themselves as sanctuaries and limited police officers' ability to inquire about immigration status.

Emigration from Mexico has fallen significantly and assumed new forms. Border enforcement has reduced illegal border crossings. The border buildup has pushed people away from urban areas to less-inhabited and more rugged terrain, increasing the number of migrant deaths. Greater law enforcement has raised the cost of crossing the border for undocumented migrants and attracted organized crime; these groups now control most human smuggling across the border. A hardened border has also created strong incentives for unauthorized immigrants to stay, or at least stay longer, in the United States rather than come and go in the traditional pattern of "circular migration."

The United States' neighbors have also recently modified their immigration laws. Canada continues to use its points system but now places a greater emphasis on specific job skills, fluency in either English or French, and prearranged employment. In 2011, Mexico passed a new immigration law to strengthen the rights of international migrants and implement new visa categories that better facilitate entry and exit. The changes are not expected to affect relations with the United States but could improve the treatment of Central American migrants in Mexico.

REGIONAL WORKFORCE

Compared to the rest of the world, North America enjoys an enviable demographic pyramid: the region's population is relatively young and fertile. North America benefits from larger families—averaging just over two children per family versus 1.6 in Europe and 1.7 in China—with the advantage coming largely from Mexico's younger population and slightly higher birth rates.[118] In fact, Mexico is currently in the middle of its "demographic bonus"—the country's working-age adults outnumber children and the elderly. By comparison, the United States' and Canada's demographics are more mature, but their age pyramids have been tempered by their relatively open immigration policies. The region's future workforce size—a fundamental factor in calculating future economic growth—also compares favorably, with 22 percent of North Americans below thirty years old, compared to 16 percent in both China and Europe.

North America has yet to make the most of its demographic advantages. It is falling behind on educating and training its young people. In the 2012 Programme for International Student Assessment (PISA) scores—an international test that measures knowledge and skills of fifteen-year-olds—Mexico ranked last among the thirty-four member countries in the OECD in math, reading, and science; Mexico was in the bottom quarter in each category when assessing the full set of sixty-four countries that took part. U.S. students ranked above the OECD average in reading but scored below the average in math and science.[119] Only Canadian students ranked among the top seven countries in each category.

This poor performance, combined with an aging population, positions North America to face severe talent shortages. By 2030, the World

Economic Forum estimates that the United States will need to add twenty-five million workers to sustain its current level of economic growth.[120] Canada, too, faces similar labor deficits; the Conference Board of Canada predicted a shortage of nearly a million workers, out of a total population of thirty-four million, by 2020.[121] Many analysts argue that Mexico is already experiencing a shortage of skilled workers, especially for advanced manufacturing.

The Task Force finds that North America's demographics could offer the region a global advantage. But regional economic integration has not been matched by integrated policies for education and workforce development. Quality education and skills development matched to economic need will be important for both national and regional economic growth and competitiveness.

U.S. POLICY

In May 2013, Presidents Obama and Peña Nieto proposed a United States-Mexico Bilateral Forum on Higher Education, Innovation, and Research to foster greater educational cooperation between Mexico and the United States, making education and academic exchanges a priority on the bilateral agenda. This forum is meant to ensure "that Mexicans and Americans work together on the cutting edge of new technologies and thinking" for the benefit of both economies.[122] It has set the ambitious goal of having one hundred thousand Mexican students studying in the United States by 2018. This project has just begun, but if the initiative proceeds as planned, it will create bilateral, rather than trilateral, mechanisms for engagement; it would fail to offer a broader vision of North America. Furthermore, the government agencies negotiating these interchanges seem disconnected from public and private institutions of higher learning. The plans do not include the institutions that would have to make hopes into realities. At a time when technological changes offer great possibilities to transform educational models, the North American countries are missing an opportunity to boost their human capital together.

Furthermore, the number of North American students who study abroad within the region remains small. In the 2012–2013 school year, some 27,000 Canadians and 14,000 Mexicans studied in the United States—only 3.3 percent and 1.7 percent of U.S. international students, respectively.[123] By comparison, there were 235,500 Chinese students,

70,627 Indian students, and 44,566 Saudi students during the same time period. U.S. students in Canada and Mexico are few and declining. From the fifth-most-popular study-abroad destination in 1998–99 (7,300 U.S. students), Mexico fell to fifteenth (3,800 students) by the 2011–2012 school year, largely due to security concerns. Academic interchanges with Canada are more common—some 10,000 U.S. students enroll individually and independently in Canadian universities (second only to U.S. students in the United Kingdom), though official study-abroad programs languish.[124] *The Task Force believes the three North American countries should promote student exchanges, which could help build a continental outlook.*

Current tools to encourage the development of a North American labor force are limited. The nonimmigrant NAFTA Professional, or Treaty NAFTA, visa was supposed to enable the movement of skilled professionals. The TN visa allows for certain Mexican and Canadian employees—those in specific professions with cross-border business responsibilities—to work for up to three years in the United States. However, these visas are underused—about 9,500 individuals received the visa in 2013.[125] This is due in part to the uncertainty of receiving the visa (the categories are ill-defined) and in part to its very temporary nature (one year, though renewable). These issues encourage skilled individuals to pursue other visa categories and green cards.

For workers who do move among NAFTA countries, the lack of recognition of degrees and credentials hinders the creation of a regional workforce. Few professions or regulated trades recognize the qualifications earned in the other NAFTA partners. Nor do they facilitate the practice of skilled trades across borders. Although a small number of professions, such as lawyers and architects, have standardized practice requirements, most professionals must essentially start over in the other countries. For instance, foreign practitioners of U.S. medicine must undergo a lengthy process to verify that their medical training matches U.S. criteria and then usually must complete a residency program in the United States, even if their competence has been verified in their previous country.

The processes to fix these issues are complex. No single U.S. authority has the power to establish official credentials; recognition is either the responsibility of an individual school, association, or state licensing board. In Canada, provincial authorities oversee credential recognition for positions in regulated industries. *The Task Force finds that this patchwork approach limits standardization, harmonization, and ultimately the transferability of degrees, which in turn creates costs for workers, businesses, and local economies. These costs are growing because the North American economies are facing labor shortages for workers who are highly skilled and have specific training in certain sectors.*

SHARED ENVIRONMENTS

The United States, Canada, and Mexico share their air, waterways, wildlife, and ecosystems. Actions in one country often have far-reaching consequences for the others. The three countries have a long history of working together on managing and conserving the region's natural resources, and of cooperating on issues such as cross-border protection of national parks and migratory wildlife.[126]

At times, shared resources have raised tensions, such as with transboundary water issues. The United States and Mexico share water from the Colorado River, which passes through seven U.S. states before crossing the border into Mexico. The Rio Grande, called the Rio Bravo in Mexico—which defines the border for 1,255 miles—has tributaries in both nations.

The frameworks for bilateral water management with Mexico go back more than a hundred years, to the first efforts to allocate levels in 1906. In 1944, the two countries created the Water Treaty to arbitrate water disputes and set new allocation levels. (The United States agreed to provide 10 percent of the Colorado River's water to Mexico, and Mexico agreed to provide the United States with one-third of the Rio Grande water originating south of the border.)[127]

In the seventy years since the 1944 treaty, the southwest border area's population, agricultural output, and manufacturing have grown dramatically. The Colorado River's water supports 15 percent of the crops in the United States and a significant portion of the agriculture in Mexico's northern states; the Colorado is now an "over-allocated basin" because the region's demand has outstripped supply.[128] In recent years, recurring droughts have further stretched water supplies. The U.S. and Mexican governments have worked to address rising demand and disputes over water quantity, quality, and conservation (including water basin and reservoir management) through various amendments to the original treaty. In regular meetings, the countries discuss issues such as Mexico's Rio Grande water debt, which has risen in recent years due to droughts.[129]

Along the northern border, the United States and Canada have managed water resources cooperatively for more than a hundred years. The International Waterways Treaty of 1909, also known as the Boundary Waters Treaty, created the International Joint Commission to settle water disputes. This framework helped manage the creation of the Saint Lawrence Seaway, a collection of locks, channels, and canals that connects the Great Lakes to the Atlantic Ocean. One of the central bilateral water issues between Canada and the United States has been pollution and invasive species in the Great Lakes, though there also have been disagreements over water diversion.

These frameworks to deal with water have been remarkably successful. They have adapted usefully to meet new challenges, such as increased salinity and droughts. Still, tensions remain. Some binational water sources, such as local aquifers, are largely unregulated. As water becomes a scarcer commodity, cooperation on water management will become even more important. *The Task Force finds that previous and current water management mechanisms have worked relatively well in addressing the use of shared resources, but it recognizes the need for continued regional cooperation because demands on limited water resources will grow.*

JOINT PREPAREDNESS FOR DISASTERS

North America's three countries have to deal with man-made and natural disasters. Deeper integration of cross-border infrastructure, such as electricity grids, provides greater resilience but also creates mutual vulnerability. Natural disasters affect communities in all three countries. The consequences of man-made disasters—including an attack on energy infrastructure, transportation networks, or health-care systems in any of the three countries—could extend far beyond national boundaries.

In recent years, North America has customized responses to meet dangers. In the wake of Hurricane Katrina, for example, both Canada and Mexico sent support teams to assist. After Hurricane Sandy, Canadian utility crews arrived in Connecticut, New York, and New Jersey to help restore power. Nevertheless, considering an increasing likelihood of disasters that will necessitate cooperative responses by one or more of the countries, the governments should assess procedural barriers to fast action in future emergencies. For example, anticipatory work could address the need for legal waivers and documentation to transport vital supplies and facilitate cross-border evacuations.

REGIONAL HEALTH

Diseases take no notice of borders. The 2009 H1N1 flu pandemic quickly spread from the United States to Mexico and then to Canada and beyond; although the death toll was relatively low, the epidemic proved costly to businesses, schools, and health care.[130] This incident highlighted the interconnected nature of North America's peoples as well as the agility of North American health agencies during the crisis. The Centers for Disease Control and Prevention (CDC) and its Canadian and Mexican counterparts worked together to identify the strain, diminish its spread, and ameliorate the symptoms of those affected. They were assisted by previous work on pandemic disease done under the now-defunct SPP.

The rapid and coordinated response reflects the generally robust cooperation among the three nations' health-care systems and the networks of research centers. The partnership also extends to the Pan American Health Organization (PAHO)—the Western Hemispheric organization for cooperation on health partnerships—with the North American countries often taking similar positions. The three countries' most recent effort is the North American Plan for Animal and Pandemic Influenza, which incorporates lessons learned and best practices from working together in order to strengthen international response capabilities for health emergencies.

North America has not developed a coordinated plan to produce and disburse vaccines and drugs. The three nations also have not created an integrated real-time database to alert governments to tainted medicines or other consumer products. Developing such a system is vital, given the interconnectedness of regional supply chains. *The Task Force recognizes the strong cooperation among the three North American countries in preparing the continent for pandemics and health emergencies. It believes the three countries can build on these foundations to integrate and streamline procedures and to ensure the continued health of North Americans.*

North America's diverse peoples are its most important resource. They are already deeply intertwined as families, workforces, and communities. Streamlining movement across the continent, capitalizing on demographic opportunities, and investing in education and training will enhance the continent's regional competitiveness in a global economy.

Recommendations

Consider the assets of North America: a population of almost half a billion; the potential for energy self-sufficiency and even exports; a wealth of human and mineral resources; peaceful and friendly neighbors; and markets for agriculture, manufacturing, services, technology, and innovation that account for more than a quarter of the world's economy. If the three democracies of North America work closely together, they will be the principal force in the world for decades to come. Canada, Mexico, and the United States have unique histories and traditions, but in combination these variances can be strengths. Together, North Americans should work to build a resilient, integrated, mutually supportive partnership that will increase their prosperity, boost security, and enhance the three countries' position globally. They can demonstrate a model of constructive integration that respects national sovereignties. For the United States in particular, North American integration can broaden, deepen, and protect the continental base for the global projection of U.S. influence and values.

It is time to put North America at the forefront of U.S. policy. The Task Force calls, first and foremost, for the U.S. government to recognize North America's importance for U.S. national security and prosperity. The Task Force urges the three countries to work together to develop and act on a common vision for North America. The guiding framework for U.S. relations with its neighbors should be: trilateral where we can, bilateral where we must.

ORGANIZING THE U.S. FEDERAL GOVERNMENT TO SHAPE A NORTH AMERICAN POLICY

To change the U.S. outlook toward its home continent, North America needs to receive continuous, not episodic, attention.

The Task Force recommends designating a senior U.S. official as the North American "champion" who will press for consistent policies across agencies and topics. Given the power relations within the U.S. government, this person would need to be the vice president, secretary of state, secretary of the treasury, or perhaps the national security adviser. The individual's interest in the role is more important than his or her bureaucratic base. The assignment would need to be backed by presidential support, including through the White House and National Security Council.

Various models have been used over the years to focus and integrate U.S. intergovernmental processes in dealing with priority relationships. The current administration looks to the vice president to lead a U.S.-Mexico High-Level Economic Dialogue. In the past, the secretary of state led a Binational Commission of cabinet officers working with Mexico. In other countries, the secretary of the treasury—or secretaries of state and treasury together—have led such efforts. Bureaucratic structures and formal meetings are less important than having a senior person who is interested and capable of driving U.S. policy toward long-term goals for North America.

The Task Force also recommends restructuring the U.S. federal government to develop a North American viewpoint and advance continental policies. The Task Force is well aware of the poor record of using governmental reorganizations to address strategic and policy problems. However, in this case, to counter the tendency to treat North America as an afterthought and to press diverse departments to work together to shape coherent policy, the Task Force believes new structures would reinforce a new continental approach.

First, the National Security Council's Directorate for Western Hemisphere Affairs should be divided into two offices, one for North America and one for South America. A North American Directorate is necessary to facilitate coordination across an especially vast interagency community that deals with Mexico and Canada. *Second, the Department of*

State's Bureau of Western Hemisphere Affairs should be divided into two bureaus as well, with one responsible for North American policy. Given the interconnectedness and interdependence of Central America and the Caribbean with North America, many Task Force members would also assign these countries to the North American units. This allocation would encourage the devotion of more serious and regular attention to these small countries, which periodically have disproportionate effects on the United States because of geographic proximity. *Other departments, for example the Department of Homeland Security, should consider complementary organizational steps to better address North America as a whole.* The Task Force notes that the Department of Defense already established NORTHCOM as a Unified Combatant Command in 2002, with Southern Command responsible for the rest of the hemisphere.

The Task Force also encourages greater U.S. congressional engagement with the Mexican congress and Canadian parliament. Increased interparliamentary exchanges could contribute to the development of a regional agenda. The Task Force would also advise the Senate Foreign Relations and House Foreign Affairs Committees to create subcommittees for North America.

ENCOURAGE STATE AND LOCAL COOPERATION

Many interactions among the three countries occur at the state and local levels. The Pacific Northwest Economic Region (PNWER) brings together policymakers and private sector representatives from the U.S. states of Alaska, Idaho, Oregon, Montana, and Washington and those from the Canadian provinces of British Columbia, Alberta, Saskatchewan, and the Yukon and Northwest Territories to promote effective cross-border policies. Interchanges between border-state governors and premiers help identify common problems and facilitate cooperative action.

The U.S. National Governors Association has separate discussions with its Mexican and Canadian counterparts. While respecting state and local prerogatives, federal governments and national associations could encourage more extensive interactions among the region's state legislators, mayors, city leaders, and other officials, such as attorneys general. *The Task Force recommends the U.S. government support interactions and possible cooperation among governors, premiers, mayors, legislators, and other officials. The three national governments could share the experience of various groups, support cooperation, and facilitate connections with others. State and local officials from across borders should be encouraged to identify emerging problems and suggest solutions. While seeking to avoid unproductive processes, the national governments might meet with cross-border groups during the annual North American Leaders' Summit.*

EXPANDING THE NORTH AMERICAN ENERGY RELATIONSHIP

Energy should become a fundamental pillar of North America's new partnership. Considering the boom in U.S. production, Mexico's historic energy sector reforms, and Canada's increased development, North America has the opportunity to become an integrated, self-sufficient energy market as well as a significant exporter of oil and natural gas. Increased and more efficient production will benefit many other industries too.

An integrated North American energy market will require significant investment in energy infrastructure, the removal of restrictions on energy trade, and enhanced mechanisms for North American cooperation. Common efforts to develop transmission networks, low-carbon energy technologies, and high environmental standards for energy production will help all three countries achieve environmental and carbon objectives.

The Task Force recommends that the North American countries develop a regional energy strategy, with full respect for sovereignty and national sensitivities.

STRENGTHEN THE NORTH AMERICAN ENERGY INFRASTRUCTURE

Restrictions on the free flow of energy create bottlenecks, inefficiencies, and unintended problems. The integration of North America's energy fields, refineries, and markets will facilitate the availability of stable and lower-cost energy.

For economic, environmental, and diplomatic reasons, the Task Force recommends that the U.S. government encourage increased energy connections with Canada and Mexico. The U.S. government should approve additional pipeline capacity, including the Keystone XL pipeline. The Task

Force also recommends that the three countries develop common rail safety standards for oil transport to reduce the chance of spills.

The electricity interconnections between the United States and Canada increase both access to supplies and grid resilience. With the opening of Mexico's electricity sector, the United States could increase electricity grid coordination along the southern border. This interconnection could also enable Mexico to benefit from the lower cost of U.S. electricity (because of natural gas development). Because the benefits of new investments in Mexico's more open oil sector could take years to appear, the gains from electric-grid partnerships could help sustain Mexican public support for the extensive energy reforms. *The Task Force recommends that the United States work with Mexico to expand cross-border electricity connections along the border (building on current links between California in the United States and Baja California in Mexico). This interconnection may require speeding permitting processes and working with local governments and the private sector to develop financing options.*

ADDRESS ENVIRONMENTAL PROTECTION AND CLIMATE CHANGE

The Task Force encourages a market-based approach to carbon pricing and the harmonization of policies across the region to minimize the shift of carbon-intensive activities. Assuming the Obama administration proceeds with the regulation of power plants' carbon dioxide (CO_2) emissions, the U.S. government should work with Canada and Mexico to make these standards consistent across North America.

North America can lead the way in continuing to reduce the amount of energy needed to generate a unit of GDP. *The Task Force urges the three nations to cooperate on the development and diffusion of technologies that promote energy conservation and reduce carbon impact.*

The Task Force suggests the creation of a North American Energy Council to provide advice to federal policymakers and highlight issues that the three independent legislative branches could address. The council would build on the call at the 2014 North American Leaders' Summit for trilateral meetings among energy ministers. It would facilitate preparation and action between the energy ministers' meetings. The council's primary responsibilities would include identifying improvements to the safety and security of cross-border energy infrastructure; areas for cooperation on environmental and safety standards; energy-efficient technologies and practices; and barriers to collaboration. This group could include representatives from the three countries' national governments, private sectors, states and provinces, civil societies, environmental groups, academia, and research communities.

END RESTRICTIONS ON U.S. OIL AND NATURAL GAS EXPORTS

U.S. law restricts the export of crude oil to countries other than Canada. U.S. exports of natural gas to countries with which the United States does not have a free trade agreement require a license from the Department of Energy. (DOE is to grant the license unless it finds the export would be contrary to the national interest.) Natural gas exports also require approval by the Federal Energy Regulatory Commission. Export restrictions run counter to the United States' goals of promoting open trade in energy, reducing the U.S. trade deficit, combating resource nationalism, and encouraging free markets. Increased exports are more likely to spur U.S. energy investment and production. North American natural gas supplies could enhance the energy security of nations dependent on supplies from Russia. Competition in the global gas markets lowers prices, supporting economic growth in important ally countries such as Japan and encouraging fuel switching from coal and oil to gas in rapidly growing economies such as China. *The Task Force proposes that the United States end restrictions on energy exports, including oil and LNG. It also urges a streamlining of the cumbersome FERC permitting process.*

ENHANCING NORTH AMERICAN ECONOMIC COMPETITIVENESS

The United States, Canada, and Mexico have all benefited from the North American Free Trade Agreement. NAFTA was a big step forward—but is not the apex of North American economic cooperation. The trilateral economic relationship should be upgraded for the twenty-first century. *The Task Force recommends working toward the free and unimpeded movement of goods and services across North America's common borders.*

FULFILL NAFTA'S TERMS

The United States should comply with all its NAFTA commitments. *The Task Force believes that the United States should fulfill its obligation to permit cross-border trucking, which has been proved safe. The Task Force urges a revision of the U.S. country-of-origin labeling of meat provisions with input from all relevant parties to reduce costs, facilitate the integration of the North American market for livestock and meat, and meet U.S. obligations. All three countries should review outstanding obligations under NAFTA and develop plans to come into full compliance with the agreement.*

REDUCE NON-TARIFF TRADE BARRIERS AND CROSS-BORDER TRANSACTION COSTS

Rules of origin have also created significant non-tariff barriers.[131] *The Task Force recommends that the three governments, working with their countries' private sectors, review and revise NAFTA's rules of origin to cut costs, boost productivity, and foster regional integration.*

Customs paperwork impedes regional trade, especially for joint production platforms through which goods may cross North America's borders multiple times before completion. *The Task Force supports the timely completion of an electronic "single window" customs system for the United States to simplify customs paperwork and eliminate the need for multiple filings. In February 2014, the North American Leaders' Summit called for such a system, and President Obama issued an executive order to achieve this goal, but execution is critical. The Task Force also encourages the United States to work with Canada and Mexico to achieve a North American "single window" to streamline regional commerce further.*

Even though NAFTA removed tariffs among the North American countries, it also exposed and inadvertently created other non-tariff barriers and transaction costs. Divergent regulations create significant obstacles to joint production and trade, raise compliance costs for businesses and their customers, have potentially harmful effects on regional health and the environment, and increase the administrative costs to governments and taxpayers. Efforts to address these costs—for example, through the U.S.-Mexico High-Level Regulatory Council and the U.S.-Canada Regulatory Cooperation Council—have not had much success.

The Task Force recommends that each council identify particular regulatory topics that are candidates for mutual recognition or harmonization. The councils could also explore continental cooperation in creating new regulations. Canadian and Mexican observers should be able to attend the meetings of the other country and the United States.

ENHANCE NORTH AMERICAN LOGISTICS AND VALUE CHAINS

Logistics are critical to North American competitiveness. To meet today's trade demands—and those of the future—North America needs to expand its capacity for legal border transit.

U.S. policymakers have inadequate knowledge about regional supply chains, making it difficult to identify steps to cut costs. *The Task Force recommends investing in data collection, results assessments, and economic return analyses for border programs and investments to better inform and direct future investment within a North American plan. Federal governments should work with the private sector and local and state governments to identify steps to enhance competitiveness.*

The Task Force commends the trilateral announcement at the February 2014 summit of the development of a North American Transportation Plan and urges the three governments to establish ambitious goals to address the infrastructure and investment factors that hinder regional competitiveness and security. The planning should work with state and local governments, the private sector, and other experts. The Task Force also encourages the U.S. Department of Transportation to consult with its Canadian and Mexican counterparts as it develops its National Freight Strategic Plan.

BUILD ON INNOVATIVE BORDER PROGRAMS

Border management within North America relies on two bilateral frameworks: the U.S.-Canada Beyond the Border arrangement and the U.S.-Mexico Twenty-First Century Border Management initiative. Over the past few years, these efforts have made significant progress. Rising enrollment in trusted-traveler programs such as NEXUS and SENTRI have reduced spikes in border delays during summers and have held wait times steady even as annual trade and transit have increased. New pilot programs to expedite trade have been launched as well.

The Task Force recommends moving toward a border-management goal of "cleared once, approved thrice." Trusted-traveler programs should become continental and reciprocal. Cargo facilitation—through programs such as the Customs-Trade Partnership Against Terrorism certification, Free and Secure Trade lanes, and preclearance pilot programs—should be expanded. The Task Force recommends a goal of reducing average wait times at the borders to thirty minutes or less, in either direction, even during peak travel times.

IMPROVE NORTH AMERICA'S PHYSICAL INFRASTRUCTURE

North America's borders should not become a choke point. The current infrastructure leaves trucks queuing for hours, undercutting the advantages of geographic proximity and trade agreements while adding unnecessary costs.

One of the bottlenecks is absence of personnel. A 2013 Government Accountability Office report estimates a deficit of more than 3,800 Customs and Border Protection officers.[132] One study shows that every additional customs officer boosts GDP by reducing wait times at border crossings.[133] *The Task Force recommends that the U.S. government review the benefit-cost data on border staffing to consider increasing the number of CBP officers at understaffed ports of entry, expanding the hours of operation at busy crossings, and harmonizing resources and times with Canadian and Mexican counterparts.*

Infrastructure limits diminish the benefits of programs such as C-TPAT certification and FAST lanes and cost the North American economies tens of billions of dollars each year. In 2011, the U.S. government estimated that a border infrastructure upgrade would require some $6 billion over the next ten years.[134]

The Task Force recommends prioritizing building lanes for primary and secondary inspections and expedited travel, and dedicated approaches for trusted-traveler programs. The U.S. government should also seek to streamline the application and certification procedures for these programs while preserving security.

More investment is needed in auxiliary roads, rail infrastructure, bridges, airports, and ports that connect cross-border flows to the larger U.S. economy. *The Task Force urges action on major infrastructure legislation, such as the Partnership to Build America Act of 2014 and Building and the Renewing Infrastructure for Development and Growth in Employment Act.*

The Task Force also urges greater support and advisory services to help local governments on innovative financing mechanisms, especially public-private partnerships. The U.S. Treasury and multilateral financial institutions already assist foreign governments with project feasibility and design, risk assessment, financial structuring, tendering, fiscal oversight, debt management, and the handling of long-term contracts; these programs could be expanded to assist state and local governments.[135] Canadian experience with the PPP Canada program, which provides the country's provinces with advice and technical financing for provincial infrastructure projects, might also be instructive.

The Task Force recommends exploring an expanded role for multilateral banks in financing border infrastructure, including possibly the North American Development Bank, the Inter-American Development Bank, and the World Bank. The NADB was created at the time of NAFTA to finance projects that address environmental or human health issues along the U.S.-Mexican border.[136] *The Task Force suggests that the NADB's mandate be expanded to include regional infrastructure investments and the U.S.-Canada border. NADB's resources may need to be expanded as well.* The Border Environment Cooperation Commission (BECC), which works with the NADB to assess the feasibility and environmental impact of potential projects, would need a complementary expansion in its mandate. *The Task Force also encourages the North American countries to approach the Inter-American Development Bank and World Bank to learn best practices for public-private partnerships, including those developed by the International Financial Corporation.*

OPEN NORTH AMERICA'S ROADS, SKIES, AND WATERWAYS

The U.S. government should seek to open up North America's roads, skies, and waterways. The United States allows Canadian and Mexican airlines to fly between U.S. cities and Canadian and Mexican cities but does not allow airlines based in Canada or Mexico to move passengers or luggage within the United States. *The Task Force recommends the negotiation of a North American "Open Skies" agreement that removes these barriers in all three countries.*

The Jones Act, passed in the 1920s, requires that all vessels moving between U.S. ports be U.S.-built, U.S.-flagged, U.S.-owned, and operated by a U.S. crew. *The Task Force recommends that the United States create a North American exception that would allow vessels that are North American–made, –flagged, and –crewed to move between and within all three nations, enabling more efficient transportation of goods. Cross-border investment within the region also could help develop a more competitive North American shipping industry.*

PROMOTE ECONOMIC TRILATERALISM

Deeper North American integration depends on the easier, faster, and more legitimate movement of people and goods. *Bilateral and dual-bilateral endeavors will and should continue, but the Task Force recommends building and expanding trilateralism over time. The goal should be trilateral where possible, bilateral where necessary.*

At the 2014 North American Leaders' Summit, the three governments announced the creation of a combined North American Trusted Traveler Program, which merges the SENTRI inspection program on the southern U.S. border and NEXUS on the northern border. *The Task Force strongly supports this trilateral trusted-traveler initiative.* The experience of the Global Entry program, which automatically enrolls participants in Transportation Security Administration PreCheck, NEXUS, and SENTRI, could be a guide.

Over the past twenty years, the three North American nations have converged considerably in their thinking on macroeconomic principles and trade. Their central banks and finance ministers have developed close partnerships, including in global forums.

The United States, Canada, and Mexico are all members of the G20, Basel Committee on Banking Supervision, IDB, World Bank, WTO, IMF, OECD, and Asia-Pacific Economic Cooperation (APEC) forum. *The Task Force recommends regular consultations among the three nations to formulate common North American economic approaches or initiatives in these multilateral bodies. They should support North American candidates for leadership posts.*

The United States was slow in supporting Canada's and Mexico's inclusion in the Trans-Pacific Partnership and has been unwilling to include its neighbors in the Transatlantic Trade and Investment Partnership negotiations. This parochialism overlooks the North American nature of many industries, as well as the significant costs that agreements might impose on regional production chains. *Although the Task Force recognizes that additional participants may add complexity to the trade negotiations, it urges the inclusion of Canada and Mexico in TTIP negotiations. The Task Force also urges the executive branch to work with Congress to pass trade promotion authority, which is crucial for the successful conclusion of both agreements.*

North America's three countries should also work together to expand partnerships with like-minded economies in Latin America. In 2012, Mexico joined Colombia, Peru, and Chile to form the Pacific Alliance. The United States and Canada already have free trade agreements with all four of these Latin American countries. *The Task Force recommends that the North American countries explore how to build on these overlapping agreements to move toward freer hemispheric trade.*

STRENGTHENING NORTH AMERICAN SECURITY

North America has come a long way from the wars of the nineteenth century to today's peaceful cooperation on common threats. This security relationship is essential to North America's future. Insecurity in any of the three countries undermines the ability to contribute and benefit from an integrated region.

PURSUE A UNIFIED APPROACH TO SECURITY

In recent years, there has been growing security cooperation along the borders and beyond. Each North American country now gathers and analyzes electronic data on all cargo shipments and travelers entering each country. The U.S.-Canada Beyond the Border and U.S.-Mexico Twenty-First Century Border Management initiatives have enabled benchmarking for risk assessment and the development of common inspection protocols for high-risk shipments and travelers entering North America. The three countries also share, usually bilaterally, information and intelligence regarding common threats, including potential terrorists and other individuals on watch lists. The interactions are usually among local law enforcement groups. The defense departments and militaries have established trilateral meetings between the

North American defense ministers; they work alongside each other at NORTHCOM's headquarters at Peterson Air Force Base.

However, North Americans are a long way from developing a unified security strategy. The United States and Canada have worked closely on security issues throughout the twentieth century. U.S. engagement with Mexico has been constrained by Mexico's resistance to a U.S. military or security presence. The United States and Canada have also had concerns about the security of information shared with some Mexican counterparts.

The Task Force recommends working toward a long-term goal of a unified security strategy for North America. This process could begin by expanding bilateral security programs to include Mexico. U.S.-Canadian programs could be incorporated into the U.S.-Mexico Twenty-First Century Border Management initiative; these efforts might include considering security risks beyond borders and developing a common assessment of risks and threats to the North American "zone." Mexico might also participate in the U.S.-Canada Shiprider program, which permits joint cross-border law enforcement operations in the maritime environment, and the Integrated Border Enforcement Teams (IBETs), which are U.S. and Canadian multiagency law enforcement groups that focus on cross-border criminal activity. These steps would require Mexico to dedicate law enforcement personnel to the security of its southern and northern borders.

To achieve a unified security strategy, the three countries should develop the confidence to share information safely between customs officers, border patrol agents, law enforcement, justice officials, and militaries.

SUPPORT MEXICAN EFFORTS TO ESTABLISH A STRONGER RULE OF LAW

The United States and Canada have a shared interest in helping Mexico strengthen its rule of law and combat organized crime. Criminal entities not only terrorize citizens but also corrupt and destroy democratic institutions. As the largest market for illegal substances and a major provider of weapons to Mexican criminal networks, the United States contributes to Mexico's problem.

The Task Force recommends that the United States, in conjunction with Canada, build upon the Mérida Initiative to support Mexican efforts to strengthen the democratic rule of law, dismantle criminal networks, contribute to the development of resilient and cohesive communities, and reduce arms smuggling and drug consumption. A common strategy should incorporate efforts to identify and disrupt criminal organizations' suppliers, distribution networks, communications, and abilities to realize profits. The United States and Canada should assist Mexico in transforming its justice system through the training of lawyers, judges, and court officials; revising of law school curricula; and supporting the use of forensic evidence. The sharing of intelligence—and training in effective use—is important. These law enforcement efforts should reach to state and local governments as well as to federal authorities.

The Task Force recognizes that the reform and professionalization of the Mexican police and criminal justice system will take time and sustained effort. *In the interim, the Task Force urges that Mexico be encouraged to continue to extradite alleged criminals to the U.S. justice system.*

The United States should also better address its own domestic challenges—including weapons trafficking, money laundering, and demand for illegal substances—which have fueled the violence in Mexico.

Various government and academic studies estimate that the majority of arms used by Mexico's criminals come from the United States and are transported illegally across the U.S.-Mexico border. *While recognizing the contentious nature of gun control and Second Amendment rights issues, the Task Force believes the United States has a responsibility to more effectively enforce existing laws to stanch the southward flow of U.S. guns.* Further, continuing to permit the sale of AR-15s and similar weapons presents a grave danger not only to Mexican security forces but also to U.S. police and law enforcement personnel. *Many Task Force members believe the U.S. government should reinstate the ban on the sale of assault weapons and high-capacity ammunition magazines.*

Billions of U.S. dollars from illicit activities are laundered within the United States.[137] The challenge is to stop the illegal flows while encouraging the legitimate financial flows that tie the nations together. *The Task Force proposes that the U.S. government strengthen domestic money laundering enforcement and work with Mexico to strengthen its anti–money laundering and asset-forfeiture laws and enforcement capabilities.*

The United States should reduce illegal drug demand and might be able to help its neighbors do the same. Studies have shown that programs for drug prevention and addiction treatment are highly cost effective. The

White House Office of National Drug Control Policy estimates that every dollar spent on prevention and treatment saves four dollars on health care and seven dollars on law enforcement and criminal justice costs.[138] *The Task Force recommends emphasizing drug prevention and treatment programs within the overall federal antinarcotics strategy.*

BOLSTER REGIONAL COOPERATION FOR SECURITY

Central America's fragile democracies, weak institutions, and growing violence represent a serious challenge for North America given the region's geographic proximity, economic and social ties, immigration patterns, and links to the international drug trade and transnational criminal organizations. These crises in Central America could destabilize neighbors and fuel illegal immigration. *The Task Force recommends greater North American cooperation in addressing the problems of Central America. A concerted effort—working with Central Americans and their governments, as well as with Colombia and Panama—is necessary to create security, good governance, the rule of law, and economic opportunity in Central America. The United States should consider the development of a sustained, multidimensional North American commitment to assist Central America along the lines of what the executive branch and Congress achieved through Plan Colombia.*

Arctic issues will require much closer cooperation with Canada. *The Task Force recommends the development of a U.S.-Canada Arctic strategy. The countries have differences to manage—such as jurisdiction over the Northwest Passage, maritime boundaries, resource utilization, and approaches to conservation. Yet strategic interests bind the two neighbors, especially relative to others. The countries should identify priorities for North American cooperation, starting with monitoring Arctic shipping channels, creating joint search-and-rescue teams, addressing territorial ownership, and sharing infrastructure and icebreakers to expand operational capacity.*

Looking forward, North America could and should contribute to global security. The United States and Canada already cooperate through the North Atlantic Treaty Organization and other multilateral bodies, as well as through United Nations peacekeeping missions.

The Task Force recommends that the United States and Canada conduct regular "policy planning" discussions with Mexico on economic and security challenges in other regions.

BUILDING A NORTH AMERICAN COMMUNITY

Immigrants and their descendants have shaped the United States. Most Americans recognize that today's immigration policies are not serving U.S. national interests and that changes are needed. The Task Force believes immigration reform would spur U.S. economic growth and entrepreneurialism, improve U.S. national security, and enable the United States to maintain its advantage as a relatively young nation. *The Task Force strongly recommends the passage of comprehensive federal immigration reform that secures U.S. borders, prevents illegal entry, provides visas on the basis of economic need, invites talented and skilled people to settle in the United States, and offers a pathway to legalization for undocumented immigrants now in the United States.*

The people of North America are critical to the future of a competitive continent. Changing economic production patterns and demographic trends will transform workforce and educational needs. *The Task Force recommends that the three nations create a North American Mobility Accord to facilitate the movement and ensure the rights of North America's workers, in particular lower-skilled guest workers and professionals on temporary assignments.*

The accord would seek to help North American employers and workers adapt flexibly to changing needs and opportunities. For example, the United States might draw on the experience of the Canada-Mexico Seasonal Agricultural Worker Program to revise the H-2A agricultural worker and H-2B seasonal worker programs. Such an approach would authorize U.S. employers to apply to the U.S. government for permission to hire guest workers; if approved, the sending country's government—Canada or Mexico—would select the workers, provide medical documents, and facilitate the workers' passage to the work sites. This model disposes of labor brokers, who vary greatly in quality. The agreement would clearly define employees' rights—in terms of wages, working conditions, health insurance, and retirement benefits—as well as the employers' obligations. The United States would be responsible for the program's oversight and enforcement within its borders, and the Canadian and Mexican governments would be responsible for guest workers within their countries. The governments may wish to begin with a pilot that could test the practical challenges of implementation.

Multinational companies should be able to move technicians, managers, experienced executives, and other professionals between facilities across borders. NAFTA created the TN visa as an expedited pathway for Canadian and Mexican workers in certain professions to work in the United States. However, the visa has been little used: there were only about 9,500 recipients of TN visas in 2013, compared to 153,000 recipients of H-1B skilled migrant visas. It appears that the more stringent TN visa rules lead qualified North Americans to apply for an H-1B visa instead.[139]

To better facilitate the movement of North American workers, the Task Force proposes that the United States, Canada, and Mexico expand and improve the TN visa category to encourage more skilled North Americans to apply. The changes—which should apply to professionals from all three countries—could include the following:

- *an expansion of the number of eligible professions*
- *the ability for TN visa holders to switch jobs within an allotted time frame, so that workers could seek another position if they lose their job*
- *an increase in the visa's annual term (subject to renewal) to three years, similar to the H-1B visa*
- *permission for TN visa holders to seek a green card (the current practice requires TN visa holders to maintain a residence in their country of origin)*
- *permission for spouses of TN visa holders to work (as is occurring with H-1B visa holders)*

North American labor integration is also inhibited by the countries' confusing, outdated, and incompatible credential systems. Qualified North American professionals—such as doctors and nurses—are often unable to practice their professions in their neighboring countries, even when the United States, Canada, and Mexico face labor shortages in those professions. *The Task Force urges the three governments to work with local and state governments and accrediting associations to streamline the recognition process for professional standards and degrees. Where possible, credentialing bodies should consider developing common criteria.*

North America should also help people who work across the continent to secure access to retirement contributions. The U.S. government has social security "totalization agreements" with Canada and more than twenty other nations; these agreements help U.S. workers accumulate years of contributions while abroad and avoid double payroll taxation by companies. *The Task Force encourages the United States to advance implementation of the U.S.-Mexico totalization agreement, which was signed in 2004 but has yet to come into effect. The United States should also work with Mexico and Canada to establish a region-wide totalization agreement so that work in any of the three countries is recognized and counted toward retirement benefits.*

EDUCATE NORTH AMERICA'S WORKFORCE

North America's peoples need high-quality education, training, and development of skills throughout their working lives. The North American countries should seek to learn from one another how innovation in education can lead to better outcomes at lower costs. For tertiary education in particular, private and public sectors across all three countries should consider the gains from common approaches with local customization. *The Task Force recommends bringing together representatives from the three countries' federal, state, and local governments, public and private schools, civil societies, and private sectors to develop a regional education and innovation strategy. This strategy should include a diversity of public and private education and technical training programs, incorporate new technologies, increase affordability, expand skills certification, and connect students to private employers. It should promote regional research through professional academic exchanges and the creation of a North American network of laboratories for basic research.*

The success of the North American community depends on the development of a common outlook by the next generation. North America's study-abroad programs lag far behind those of other regions. *The Task Force recommends an expanded interchange among North American young people. This effort might build on existing programs—leveraging, implementing, and increasing current study abroad, including the U.S. State Department's 100,000 Strong in the Americas initiative and Fulbright programs, Canada's International Education Strategy, and the Mexican Proyecta 100,000, a recent initiative to support foreign study.*

PROTECT THE SHARED CONTINENT

Regional Disasters
Proximity and shared infrastructure create shared vulnerabilities. Joint emergency responses have improved—for instance, in earthquake and fault zones—thanks to regional monitoring, early warning systems, and quick-response training. Unfortunately, regional barriers continue

to hinder contingency planning and cooperation. The multiplicity of actors complicates the sharing of information. Bureaucratic procedures impede swift and flexible responses. Canadian firefighters who previously came to the aid of border towns in Vermont and New York have been thwarted by new border checks.

The Task Force recommends enabling flexible responses to emergencies. Legal waivers, recognition of expert credentials, pre-clearance for the transport of crucial supplies, and evacuation plans enable neighbors to assist one another at critical moments.

Cybersecurity
The control functions for North America's shared power grids, water lines, and other infrastructure are increasingly online: breaches could produce large-scale devastation across borders. Cyber failures in one country could have ripple effects on neighbors and cross-border production. Cyber safety should address the risks of both a catastrophic attack and small-scale hacking that tampers with or steals information.

The Task Force recommends that the United States, Canada, and Mexico set baseline standards for cyber protection. This work could start with the evaluation of vulnerabilities and sharing best practices among governments, private sectors, universities, and others. The three countries should promulgate jointly the measures identified in cybersecurity frameworks, such as the Critical Security Controls and the U.S. Department of Homeland Security's Continuous Diagnostics and Mitigation program. North America can prevent or thwart 80 to 90 percent of all known cyberattacks by emphasizing basic cyber safety practices, known as "cyber hygiene."

To ensure closer cooperation and understanding in this dynamic area, the United States, Canada, and Mexico should establish a standing consultative mechanism through their national Computer Emergency Readiness Teams (CERTs). These teams need representatives from the private as well as public sectors. The consultative mechanism could share information on threats, develop standardized response protocols, and conduct after-action evaluations.

The Task Force urges that postcrisis evaluations of both man-made and natural disasters—which are common within the U.S. government—incorporate consultations with Canada and Mexico.

MAINTAIN NORTH AMERICA'S ENVIRONMENT
AND HEALTH

The air, water, and wildlife of the North American community are its common heritage and natural culture. The three North American countries have a long history of working together to manage shared natural resources, with some efforts begun over a century ago.

Water
The three countries should build on their long history of cooperation to promote water stewardship. *The Task Force urges that the institutions charged with water management address current issues, such as the diversion of water from one watershed to another, water quota allocations, and the introduction of invasive alien species that threaten ecosystems and commercial industries.*

Health
Pathogens pose potentially devastating threats to the populations of North America. The continent has a history of robust cooperation between its centers for disease control, research laboratories, and representatives with multilateral organizations such as the Pan American Health Organization. *The Task Force recommends that the United States, Canada, and Mexico develop protocols and agreements for the production and sharing of drugs and equipment to prepare for future epidemics.*

The United States and its neighbors should establish a real-time exchange of information about fraudulent drug investigations and outbreaks, similar to that which exists between the United States and the European Union, to better ensure the health and safety of North America's peoples.

Conclusion: The New World of North America

North America was once called the New World. The people, resources, and ingenuities of the continent shaped the histories of the Old World—East and West. Today, North America is the home of almost five hundred million people who have the good fortune and potential to influence global affairs in the coming centuries as well. To do so, the three countries should first recognize their common cultures and interests. Often their publics are ahead of the governments in seeing the interconnections.

This is the moment for the U.S. government to break old foreign policy patterns and recognize the importance of its own neighborhood. A more integrated, dynamic, safe, and prosperous North America will secure the U.S. continental base and strengthen its global reach.

Additional or Dissenting Views

The Task Force report identifies a gap in U.S. foreign policy that needs to be rectified. I support the report's general thrust and most of its specific recommendations but would add two comments.

First, with regard to strengthening North American security, the report appropriately identifies the threat that Mexico-based drug cartels—large, powerful, and corrupt criminal organizations—pose to Mexican institutions and to the United States and Canada. The report recommends the adoption of a common strategy to dismantle the cartels but does not describe what it might entail. As demonstrated in Colombia in the 1990s, a comprehensive law-enforcement strategy can successfully destroy large criminal organizations, but it must go beyond locating and removing the organization's kingpin. This strategy should aim to weaken and implode the organization itself by disrupting its cash flow, distribution, and supply chains and confiscating its assets.

Second, the report suggests that North American countries adopt a "market-based approach to carbon pricing." I am dubious of any strategy that might harm the North American economies. Encouraging market-based carbon pricing, which requires a regulatory scheme, gets into questions of what measures can reduce warming and at what cost. Implementing such a scheme only makes sense with broad international consensus, although even then there is the potential for large-scale fraud and noncompliance.

Robert C. Bonner

I share the Task Force's enthusiasm for the large economic and geopolitical benefits of the rapid growth in North America's oil and gas production, which stem from technological innovations in the extraction of hydrocarbons from shale. I agree that North American regulations should be modernized to reflect this transformed energy landscape, including to enable new energy production to come to market and to ensure it is produced and transported safely.

However, I believe the Task Force's recommendations do not adequately convey the importance of much more aggressive policy measures that the United States, Canada, and Mexico need to undertake to combat the potentially severe consequences of climate change—even as we take advantage of newfound domestic hydrocarbon resources on which our economies will rely for years to come.

In addressing the environmental effects of a North American hydrocarbon renaissance, the report notes that increased carbon emissions contribute to climate change and can impose significant costs. Regardless of the future of North American oil and gas production, however, the United States, Canada, and Mexico need to adopt strong market-based policies to internalize the social costs associated with greenhouse-gas emissions and reduce emissions at the lowest cost. These measures can be even more effective if the three nations coordinate closely on climate policy.

Although the report rightly notes that U.S. emissions have fallen to the lowest levels in two decades, driven in significant part by low-cost natural gas displacing coal for power generation, it is important to acknowledge that market forces alone will not drive necessary emissions reductions. Indeed, U.S. greenhouse-gas emissions rose in 2013, as natural gas prices increased and coal regained market share.

On the topic of infrastructure, I disagree with the report's finding that government policy and permitting requirements are significantly undermining the economic benefits of the North American energy renaissance by stymieing investment in infrastructure to bring energy to market. Aside from some exceptions, most notably the long-delayed Keystone XL pipeline to Canada, capital markets have responded to the energy boom, and the midstream sector is growing rapidly. Of the 4,300 miles of crude and product pipelines built around the world in 2014, more than 3,300 miles are in the United States. Of course, government should strive to reduce red tape and can often act more quickly, but pipeline projects are often delayed or shelved for more significant reasons than policy, including cost, interest-group lawsuits, and the flexibility of rail. Although government regulations need to be smart, well-targeted and effective regulations are necessary. They not only protect public health and safety, but also build the public trust necessary for the North American hydrocarbon boom to continue.

Additionally, a reader may come away with the incorrect impression that U.S. liquefied natural gas exports are being limited by the relatively few permits granted to date by the Department of Energy and the Federal Energy Regulatory Commission. To date, the DOE has conditionally approved 10.5 billion cubic feet per day of LNG exports, a volume exceeding that of Qatar, which is currently the largest LNG exporter in the world. More important, the DOE recently changed its export-approval policy, removing the conditional-authorization requirement so that the department may consider for final authorization only the most viable projects—those able to finance completion of the FERC authorization process. This allows commercial considerations, rather than government permitting, to determine which LNG projects are built. Obtaining FERC authorization is a costly process, but also a predictable one for viable projects to complete. FERC has approved four projects, with several more permits expected in the next six to nine months. And the DOE continues to issue authorizations, most recently giving two more projects final approval on September 10, 2014.

Jason Eric Bordoff

I endorse the Task Force report and its goals of regional integration, but I would stress the importance of addressing social and economic inequality both among and within the three nations. The structural differences in opportunities for individuals, families, and communities limit the spread of benefits and restrict the most vulnerable from joining the economic mainstream or contributing to growth. Economic integration in North America magnifies the importance of a level economic playing field as workforces become increasingly interdependent. Related topics such as financial inclusion, resilience among the poorest, and women's economic empowerment should prevail in policy discussions focused on inequality. Education, discussed in this report, is also a good place to start, and policymakers should ensure that improvements in access and quality incorporate the needs of the lowest income groups in all three nations. More equal educational opportunity will help societies understand the benefits of the deepening ties among their countries and will enhance each individual's ability to participate and compete in a globalized world.

Maria Otero

Endnotes

1. Frank Graves, Robert Pastor, and Miguel Basáñez, "The NAFTA Promise and the North American Reality," presentation to the Center for North American Studies and the Institutions, Law, and Security Center, October 31, 2013, http://www.american.edu/sis/cnas/upload/3_a_2013CNAS_Survey_Summary_Results.pdf.
2. Five Eyes is an alliance of intelligence operations that includes the United States, Canada, Australia, New Zealand, and the United Kingdom; Paul Farrell, "History of 5-Eyes—Explainer," *Guardian*, December 2, 2013, http://www.theguardian.com/world/2013/dec/02/history-of-5-eyes-explainer.
3. U.S. Energy Information Administration, "AEO2014 Early Release Overview," December 16, 2013, http://www.eia.gov/forecasts/aeo/er/early_production.cfm.
4. Grant Smith, "US Seen as Biggest Oil Producer After Overtaking Saudi Arabia," Bloomberg, July 4, 2014, http://www.bloomberg.com/news/2014-07-04/u-s-seen-as-biggest-oil-producer-after-overtaking-saudi.html.
5. U.S. Energy Information Administration, "International Energy Statistics," http://www.eia.gov/cfapps/ipdbproject/iedindex3.cfm?tid=3&pid=26&aid=1&cid=regions&syid=2005&eyid=2013&unit=BCF.
6. Energy Resources Conservation Board, "ERCB Report Indicates Largest Conventional Crude Oil Production and Reserves Increase in Decades," May 8, 2013, http://www.aer.ca/documents/news-releases/NR2013-09.pdf; Statistics Canada, "Energy Statistics Handbook," http://www.statcan.gc.ca/pub/57-601-x/57-601-x2012001-eng.pdf; Canadian Energy Research Institute, "CERI Commodity Report—Crude Oil," January-February 2014, http://www.ceri.ca/images/stories/CERI_Crude_Oil_Report_-_January-February_2014.pdf.
7. U.S. Energy Information Administration, "Shale Oil and Shale Gas Resources," June 10, 2013, http://www.eia.gov/todayinenergy/detail.cfm?id=11611.
8. U.S. Energy Information Administration, "Technically Recoverable Shale Oil and Shale Gas Resources: An Assessment of 137 Shale Formations in 41 Countries Outside the United States," June 2013, http://www.eia.gov/analysis/studies/worldshalegas.
9. EFE, "México Prevé Aumento de 40 Por Ciento en Producción de Crudo tras Reforma Energética," March 6, 2014, http://mexico.servidornoticias.com/2229_economia/2444694_mexico-preve-aumento-de-40-por-ciento-en-produccion-de-crudo-tras-reforma-energetica.html.
10. BP, "BP Energy Outlook 2013," January 2013, http://www.bp.com/content/dam/bp/pdf/statistical-review/BP_World_Energy_Outlook_booklet_2013.pdf.
11. BP, "BP Statistical Review of World Energy 2014," June 2014, http://www.bp.com/content/dam/bp/pdf/Energy-economics/statistical-review-2014/BP-statistical-review-of-world-energy-2014-full-report.pdf.
12. U.S. Department of Energy, "Progress Report: Advancing Solar Energy Across America," February 12, 2014, http://www.energy.gov/articles/progress-report-advancing-solar-energy-across-america.

13. U.S. Energy Information Administration, "Mexico: Background," October 17, 2012, http://www.eia.gov/countries/cab.cfm?fips=MX; Pike Research, "Wind Energy Outlook for North America," Pike Research, accessed December 5, 2013, http://www.navigantresearch.com/research/wind-energy-outlook-for-north-america.

14. U.S. Energy Information Administration, "Exports by Destination," accessed March 4, 2014, http://www.eia.gov/dnav/pet/pet_move_expc_a_EPC0_EEX_mbblpd_a.htm.

15. This includes coal, crude oil, fuel oil, petroleum products, natural gas liquids, natural gas, and nuclear fuel materials. U.S. Census Bureau, "U.S. Imports to Canada by 5-digit End-Use Code, 2004–2013," accessed June 13, 2014, http://www.census.gov/foreign-trade/statistics/product/enduse/imports/c1220.html; U.S. Census Bureau, "U.S. Exports to Canada by 5-digit End-Use Code, 2004–2013," accessed June 13, 2014, http://www.census.gov/foreign-trade/statistics/product/enduse/exports/c1220.html.

16. U.S. Energy Information Administration, "U.S. Imports by Country of Origin," accessed March 19, 2014, http://www.eia.gov/dnav/pet/pet_move_impcus_a2_nus_ep00_im0_mbblpd_a.htm.

17. U.S. Census Bureau, "U.S. Imports from Mexico," accessed March 19, 2014, http://www.census.gov/foreign-trade/statistics/product/enduse/imports/c2010.html; U.S. Census Bureau, "U.S. Exports to Mexico," U.S. Census Bureau, accessed March 19, 2014, http://www.census.gov/foreign-trade/statistics/product/enduse/exports/c2010.html.

18. Ibid.

19. U.S. Energy Information Administration, "U.S. Natural Gas Imports," accessed March 20, 2014, http://www.eia.gov/dnav/ng/ng_move_impc_s1_a.htm; U.S. Energy Information Administration, "Canada: Background," U.S. Energy Information Administration, December 10, 2012, http://www.eia.gov/countries/cab.cfm?fips=CA.

20. The EIA predicts that U.S. gas exports to Mexico will rise more than fourfold by 2025.

21. "Mexico's Pemex Opens Contract Bids for Ramones Gas Pipeline Project," Reuters, May 13, 2013, http://www.reuters.com/article/2013/05/14/mexico-gas-idUSL2N0DV06820130514.

22. IHS, "Total 2012 Upstream Oil and Gas Spending to Reach Record Level of Nearly $1.3 Trillion; Set to Exceed $1.6 Trillion by 2016, IHS Study Says," April 30, 2012, http://press.ihs.com/press-release/energy-power/total-2012-upstream-oil-and-gas-spending-reach-record-level-nearly-13-tri.

23. Harold L. Sirkin, Michael Zinser, and Justin Rose, "The Shifting Economics of Global Manufacturing: How Cost Competitiveness Is Changing Worldwide," Boston Consulting Group, August 2014, https://www.bcgperspectives.com/Images/The_Shifting_Economics_of_Global_Manufacturing_Aug_2014_tcm80-165933.pdf.

24. Steve Strongin, Jeff Currie, and Daniel Quigley, "Unlocking the economic potential of North America's energy resources," Goldman Sachs, June 2014, http://www.goldmansachs.com/our-thinking/our-conferences/north-american-energy-summit/unlocking-the-economic-potential-of-north-americas.pdf.

25. Susan Lund, James Manyika, Scott Nyquist, Lenny Mendonca, and Sreenivas Ramaswamy, "Game Changers: Five Opportunities for U.S. Growth and Renewal," McKinsey Global Institute, July 2013, http://www.mckinsey.com/insights/americas/us_game_changers; IHS, "America's New Energy Future: The Unconventional Oil and Gas Revolution and the U.S. Economy," September 2013, http://www.ihs.com/images/Americas-New-Energy-Future-Mfg-Renaissance-Main-Report-Sept13.pdf; Edward Morse, Aakash Doshi, Eric Lee, Seth Kleinman, Daniel Ahn, and Anthony Yuen, "Energy 2020: North America, the New Middle East," Citi, March 20, 2012, http://www.morganstanleyfa.com/public/projectfiles/ce1d2d99-c133-4343-8ad0-43aa1da63cc2.pdf.

26. Ibid.

27. "From Sunset to New Dawn," *Economist*, November 16, 2013, http://www.economist. com/news/business/21589870-capitalists-not-just-greens-are-now-questioning-how-significant-benefits-shale-gas-and.

28. Petroleum Labour Market Information, "The Decade Ahead: Labour Market Outlook to 2022 for Canada's Oil and Gas Industry," May 2013, http://www.iecbc.ca/sites/ default/files/Enform%20Petroleum%20Labour%20Market%20Information%20 canada_labour_market_outlook_to_2022_report_may_2013.pdf, p. 3.

29. Instituto Mexicano para la Competitividad, "Nos Cambiaron el Mapa: Mexico ante la Revolucíon Energética del Siglo XXI," July 2013, http://imco.org.mx/wp-content/ uploads/2013/07/Presentaci%C3%B3nIMCOFinal-CORREGIDO.pdf.

30. IHS, "America's New Energy Future: The Unconventional Oil and Gas Revolution and the Economy—Volume 3: A Manufacturing Renaissance," http://www.ihs.com/ info/ecc/a/americas-new-energy-future-report-vol-3.aspx.

31. IHS, "America's New Energy Future: The Unconventional Oil and Gas Revolution and the U.S. Economy," September 2013, http://www.ihs.com/images/Americas-New-Energy-Future-Mfg-Renaissance-Main-Report-Sept13.pdf.

32. Steve Strongin, Jeff Currie, and Daniel Quigley, "Unlocking the economic potential of North America's energy resources" Goldman Sachs, June 2014, http://www. goldmansachs.com/our-thinking/our-conferences/north-american-energy-summit/ unlocking-the-economic-potential-of-north-americas.pdf.

33. ConocoPhillips Alaska, "Kenai LNG Exports," http://alaska.conocophillips.com/ what-we-do/natural-gas/lng/Pages/kenai-lng-exports.aspx.

34. BP, "Natural gas prices," http://www.bp.com/en/global/corporate/about-bp/energy-economics/statistical-review-of-world-energy/review-by-energy-type/natural-gas/ natural-gas-prices.html.

35. U.S. Department of Energy, "Applications Received by DOE/FE to Export Domestically Produced LNG from the Lower-48 States," September 10, 2014, http://energy.gov/sites/ prod/files/2014/09/f18/Summary%20of%20LNG%20Export%20Applications.pdf.

36. Federal Energy Regulatory Commission, "North American LNG Import/Export Terminals: Approved," August 15, 2014, http://www.ferc.gov/industries/gas/indus-act/ lng/lng-approved.pdf; Federal Energy Regulatory Commission, "North American LNG Import/Export Terminals: Proposed," August 15, 2014, http://www.ferc.gov/ industries/gas/indus-act/lng/lng-export-proposed.pdf.

37. Ernest Scheyder, "Exclusive: Bakken Flaring Burns More Than $100 Million a Month," Reuters, July 29, 2013, http://www.reuters.com/article/2013/07/29/ us-bakken-flaring-idUSBRE96S05320130729.

38. Associated Press, "Crude Oil Shipments by Rail Increased 83 Percent in 2013," *New York Times*, March 13, 2014, http://www.nytimes.com/2014/03/14/business/crude-oil-shipments-by-rail-increased-83-percent-in-2013.html.

39. Institute for Energy Research, "Oil Shipments by Rail, Truck, and Barge Up Substantially," September 9, 2013, http://www.instituteforenergyresearch.org/2013/09/09/ oil-shipments-by-rail-truck-and-barge-up-substantially.

40. Transporting crude by rail results in a higher number of spills but releases less crude overall. John Kemp, "Pipelines vs. Rail for Moving Oil Safely—A Close Call," Reuters, July 10, 2013, http://www.reuters.com/article/2013/07/10/column-kemp-canada-train-idUSL6N0FG26C20130710; John Frittelli, Paul W. Parfomak, Jonathan L. Ramseur, Anthony Andrews, Robert Pirog, and Michael Ratner, "U.S. Rail Transportation of Crude Oil: Background and Issues for Congress," Congressional Research Service, May 5, 2014, https://www.fas.org/sgp/crs/misc/R43390.pdf.

41. Marc Humphries, "U.S. Crude Oil and Natural Gas Production in Federal and Non-Federal Areas," Congressional Research Service, April 10, 2014, http:// energycommerce.house.gov/sites/republicans.energycommerce.house.gov/files/

20140410CRS-US-crude-oil-natural-gas-production-federal-non-federal-areas.pdf.

42. U.S. Census Bureau, "U.S. Trade in Goods with Mexico," accessed March 19, 2014, http://www.census.gov/foreign-trade/balance/c2010.html; U.S. Census Bureau, "U.S. Trade in Goods with Canada," accessed March 19, 2014, http://www.census.gov/foreign-trade/balance/c1220.html.

43. U.S. Census Bureau, "U.S. Trade in Goods with China," accessed December 4, 2013, http://www.census.gov/foreign-trade/balance/c5700.html; U.S. Census Bureau, "U.S. Trade in Goods with European Union," accessed December 4, 2013, http://www.census.gov/foreign-trade/balance/c0003.html.

44. Secretaria de Economía, "Comercio Exterior: Información Estadística y Arancelaria," accessed December 4, 2013, http://www.economia.gob.mx/comunidad-negocios/comercio-exterior/informacion-estadistica-y-arancelaria; Statistics Canada, "Canadian International Merchandise Trade Database," accessed December 4, 2013, http://www5.statcan.gc.ca/cimt-cicm/home-accueil?lang=eng.

45. U.S. Census Bureau, "2011 Exports by Company Employment Size to World Areas and Selected Countries," accessed December 4, 2013, http://www.census.gov/foreign-trade/Press-Release/edb/2011/exh5a.pdf.

46. Gary Clyde Hufbauer, Cathleen Cimino, and Tyler Moran, "NAFTA at 20: Misleading Charges and Positive Achievements," Peterson Institute for International Economics, May 2014, http://www.piie.com/publications/pb/pb14-13.pdf, p. 2.

47. The main export destination for Alaska is China; for Connecticut is France; for Delaware is Belgium; for Washington, DC, is the United Arab Emirates; for Florida is Brazil; for Hawaii is Australia; for Louisiana is China; for Mississippi is Panama; for Nevada is Switzerland; for Puerto Rico is Belgium; for South Carolina is China; for Utah is Hong Kong; and for Washington is China. U.S. Census Bureau, "Foreign Trade," accessed May 22, 2014, http://www.census.gov/foreign-trade/statistics/state/data/pr.html.

48. Robert Koopman, William Powers, Zhi Wang, and Shang-Jin Wei, "Give Credit Where Credit is Due: Tracing Value Added In Global Production Chains," National Bureau of Economic Research, September 2010, http://www.nber.org/papers/w16426.pdf, p. 38.

49. U.S. Census Bureau, "U.S. Trade in Goods with Mexico," accessed March 19, 2014, http://www.census.gov/foreign-trade/balance/c2010.html; U.S. Census Bureau, "U.S. Trade in Goods with Canada," U.S. Census Bureau, accessed April 28, 2014, https://www.census.gov/foreign-trade/balance/c1220.html#2013; U.S. Census Bureau, "U.S. Trade in Goods with China," accessed March 19, 2014, http://www.census.gov/foreign-trade/balance/c1220.html.

50. World Trade Organization, "International Trade Database," accessed December 4, 2013, http://stat.wto.org/Home/WSDBHome.aspx?Language=E.

51. Ibid.

52. Ibid.

53. M. Angeles Villarreal and Ian F. Fergusson, "NAFTA at 20: Overview and Trade Effects," Congressional Research Service, April 28, 2014, http://fas.org/sgp/crs/row/R42965.pdf, p. 28.

54. Organization for Economic Cooperation and Development, "FDI Positions by Partner Country," accessed August 11, 2014, http://www.oecd.org/corporate/mne/statistics.htm.

55. Bureau of Economic Analysis, "Foreign Direct Investment in the U.S.: Balance of Payments and Direct Investment Position Data," U.S. Department of Commerce, accessed July 6, 2014, https://www.bea.gov/international/di1fdibal.htm.

56. World Trade Organization, "Time Series on international trade," accessed December 4, 2013, http://stat.wto.org/Home/WSDBHome.aspx?Language=E.

57. Hufbauer, Cimino, and Moran, "NAFTA at 20: Misleading Charges and Positive Achievements."

58. John J. Audley, Demetrios G. Papademetriou, Sandra Polaski, and Scott Vaughan, "NAFTA's Promise and Reality: Lessons From Mexico for the Hemisphere," Carnegie Endowment for International Peace, 2004, http://carnegieendowment.org/files/nafta1.pdf; Pierre S. Pettigrew, Robert B. Zoellick, and Luis Ernesto Derbez, "NAFTA at Eight: A Foundation of Economic Growth," Office of the U.S. Trade Representative, 2002, http://www.ustr.gov/archive/assets/Trade_Agreements/Regional/NAFTA/asset_upload_file374_3603.pdf.

59. Cynthia English, "Opinion Briefing: North American Free Trade Agreement," Gallup, December 12, 2008, http://www.gallup.com/poll/113200/opinion-briefing-north-american-free-trade-agreement.aspx.

60. Chicago Council on Global Affairs, "Anxious Americans Seek a New Direction in United States Foreign Policy," 2008, http://www.thechicagocouncil.org/UserFiles/File/POS_Topline%20Reports/POS%202008/2008%20Public%20Opinion%202008_US%20Survey%20Results.pdf, p. 21.

61. Conversation with Bruce Stokes of the Pew Research Center comparing an April 2014 Pew attitudes survey on TTIP, "Support in Principle for U.S.-EU Trade Pact," to attitudes on NAFTA approval.

62. Gianmarco I.P. Ottaviano and Giovanni Peri, "Rethinking the Effects of Immigration on Wages," National Bureau of Economic Research, August 2006, http://www.nber.org/papers/w12497.

63. The Bureau of Labor Statistics only tracked job outsourcing until 2004, after which it changed its categorizations. Sharon P. Brown, "Mass Layoff Statistics Data in the United States and Domestic and Overseas Relocation," Bureau of Labor Statistics, December 13–14, 2004, http://www.bls.gov/mls/mlsrelocation.pdf.

64. Hufbauer, Cimino, and Moran, "NAFTA at 20: Misleading Charges and Positive Achievements."

65. This is using the net cost method of measuring rules of origin. Villarreal and Fergusson, "NAFTA at 20: Overview and Trade Effects," p. 6.

66. Robert Pastor, *The North American Idea: A Vision of a Continental Future* (New York: Oxford University Press, 2011), p. 134.

67. U.S. Customs and Border Protection, "Automated Commercial Environment (ACE)/International Trade Data System (ITDS)," accessed May 7, 2014, http://www.cbp.gov/sites/default/files/documents/ACEopedia%20March%202014%20v1.pdf.

68. The White House, "Executive Order—Streamlining the Export/Import Process for America's Businesses," February 19, 2014, http://www.whitehouse.gov/the-press-office/2014/02/19/executive-order-streamlining-exportimport-process-america-s-businesses.

69. Pastor, *The North American Idea*, p. 135.

70. Canada-U.S. Regulatory Cooperation Council, "Canada-U.S. Regulatory Cooperation Council (RCC) Stakeholder Dialogue Session," June 20, 2013, http://www.trade.gov/rcc/meeting-of-canada-us-rcc-06192020213.asp.

71. Canada-U.S. Regulatory Cooperation Council "Canada-U.S. Regulatory Cooperation Council Joint Action Plan Progress Report to Leaders," December 2012, http://www.trade.gov/rcc/documents/rcc-progress-report-release.pdf; U.S.-Mexico Regulatory Cooperation Council, "U.S.-Mexico Regulatory Cooperation Council Progress Report to Leaders," August 15, 2013, http://www.trade.gov/hlrcc.

72. Robert J. Carbaugh, "NAFTA and the US-Mexican Trucking Dispute," *Journal of International and Global Economic Studies* vol. 4, no. 1, June 2011, http://www2.southeastern.edu/orgs/econjournal/index_files/JIGES%20JUNE%202011%20NAFTA%20and%20the%20U.S.-Mexican%20Trucking%20Dispute.pdf.

73. Beatriz Leycegui, *Reflexiones Sobre La Politica Comercial Internacional de Mexico 2006–2012* (Mexico City: ITAM, Secretaría de Economía, Miguel Ángel Porrua, 2012), pp. 387–90.

74. John Frittelli, "Status of Mexican Trucks in the United States Frequently Asked Questions," Congressional Research Service, January 3, 2014, http://fas.org/sgp/crs/misc/R41821.pdf.

75. Pastor, *The North American Idea*, pp. 127–28.

76. Mikhail Pavlov, "Meeting Land Port of Entry Modernization Needs in Constrained Budgetary Environment," presentation to the Joint Working Committee, Customs and Border Protection, Department of Homeland Security, March 14–15, 2012, http://texasbmps.com/wp-content/uploads/downloads/2011/11/Pavlov_JWC-CBP-Presentation1.pdf, p. 3.

77. U.S. Government Accountability Office, "CBP Action Needed to Improve Wait Time Data and Measure Outcomes of Trade Facilitation Efforts," July 2013, http://www.gao.gov/assets/660/656140.pdf; Erik Lee, Christopher E. Wilson, Francisco Lara-Valencia, Carlos A. de la Parra, Rick Van Schoik, Kristofer Patron-Soberano, Eric L. Olson, and Andrew Selee, "The State of the Border Report," Woodrow Wilson Mexico Institute, El Colegio de la Frontera Norte, and the North American Center for Transborder Studies, May 2013, http://www.wilsoncenter.org/sites/default/files/mexico_state_of_border_0.pdf.

78. American Society of Civil Engineers, "2013 Report Card for America's Infrastructure," March 2013, http://www.infrastructurereportcard.org/a/documents/2013-Report-Card.pdf.

79. Robert Z. Lawrence, Margareta Drzeniek Hanouz, and Sean Doherty, "Global Enabling Trade Report 2012," World Economic Forum, 2012, http://www3.weforum.org/docs/GETR/2012/GlobalEnablingTrade_Report.pdf.

80. Klaus Schwab, *Global Competitiveness Report 2013–2014*, World Economic Forum, 2013, http://www3.weforum.org/docs/WEF_GlobalCompetitivenessReport_2013–14.pdf.

81. Ian F. Fergusson, William H. Cooper, Remy Jurenas, and Brock R. Williams, "The Trans-Pacific Partnership Negotiations and Issues for Congress," Congressional Research Service, December 13, 2013, http://www.fas.org/sgp/crs/row/R42694.pdf, p. 1.

82. U.S. Border Patrol, "Nationwide Illegal Alien Apprehensions Fiscal Years 1925–2013," accessed December 4, 2013, http://www.cbp.gov/linkhandler/ cgov/border_security/border_patrol/usbp_statistics/usbp_fy12_stats/appr_stats_1925_2012.ctt/appr_stats_1925_2012.pdf.

83. Instituto Nacional de Estadística y Geografía, "Encuesta Nacional de victimización y Percepción Sobre Seguridad Pública 2013," September 30, 2013, http://www.inegi.org.mx/inegi/contenidos/espanol/prensa/Boletines/Boletin/Comunicados/Especiales/2013/septiembre/comunica15.pdf.

84. U.S. Border Patrol, "Border Patrol Staffing by Fiscal Year", accessed March 21, 2014, http://www.cbp.gov/sites/default/files/documents/U.S.%20Border%20Patrol%20Fiscal%20Year%20Staffing%20Statistics%201992-2013.pdf.

85. U.S. Border Patrol, "Enacted Border Patrol Program Budget by Fiscal Year," accessed March 21, 2014, http://www.cbp.gov/sites/default/files/documents/BP%20Budget%20History%201990-2013.pdf.

86. U.S. Government Accountability Office, "Secure Border Initiative Fence Construction Costs," January 29, 2009, http://www.gao.gov/new.items/d09244r.pdf, p. 1.

87. U.S. 104th Congress, "Public Law 104–208," September 30, 1996, p. 559, http://www.dol.gov/ocfo/media/regs/FFMIA.pdf.

88. U.S. 110th Congress, "Mérida Initiative to Combat Illicit Narcotics and Reduce

Organized Crime Authorization Act of 2008," June 11, 2008, https://www.govtrack.us/congress/bills/110/hr6028/text.

89. U.S. Bureau of Transportation Statistics, "Border Crossing/Entry Data: Query Detailed Statistics," accessed March 24, 2014, http://transborder.bts.gov/programs/international/transborder/TBDR_BC/TBDR_BCQ.html.

90. Ibid.

91. Fredrik Dahl, "Mexico 'Systematically Weakening' Crime Cartels: Minister," Reuters, October 15, 2012, http://www.reuters.com/article/2012/10/15/us-crime-mexico-idUSBRE89E0WU20121015.

92. Centro de Investigación para el Desarrollo, A.C., "Reporte de Hallazgos Para el Seguimiento y la Evaluación de la Implementación y Operación del Nuevo Sistema de Justicia Penal en México," 2013, http://cidac.org/esp/uploads/1/Hallazgos_implementacio__n_Reforma_Penal.pdf.

93. U.S. Department of State, "Congressional Budget Justification: Foreign Assistance FY2014," accessed April 28, 2014, http://www.state.gov/documents/organization/224071.pdf; U.S. Department of State, "Congressional Budget Justification: Foreign Assistance FY2013," accessed April 28, 2014, http://www.state.gov/documents/organization/185016.pdf; U.S. Department of State, "Congressional Budget Justification: Foreign Assistance FY2012," accessed April 28, 2014, http://www.state.gov/documents/organization/158269.pdf.

94. Clare Ribando Seelke and Kristin Finklea, "U.S.-Mexican Security Cooperation: The Mérida Initiative and Beyond," Congressional Research Service, April 9, 2014, http://fas.org/sgp/crs/row/R41349.pdf, p. 1.

95. Canadian International Development Platform, "Canada's Foreign Aid 2012," North-South Institute, accessed December 4, 2013, http://cidpnsi.ca/blog/portfolio/canadas-foreign-aid.

96. There is considerable debate surrounding the percentage of weapons recovered in Mexico that can be traced to the United States. In 2009, the Government Accountability Office reported that 87 percent of weapons seized in Mexico from 2004 to 2008 originated in the United States. However, these figures include only the weapons that the Mexican government provided to the Bureau of Alcohol, Tobacco, Firearms, and Explosives, leading some to question Mexico's process of selecting which guns to trace. In 2013, the ATF traced 15,083 guns, with 10,488 originating in the United States (69.5 percent); another 20.1 percent were not traced to the United States, and 10.4 percent remained undetermined. U.S. Government Accountability Office, "Firearms Trafficking: U.S. Efforts to Combat Arms Trafficking to Mexico Face Planning and Coordination Challenges," June 2009, http://www.gao.gov/new.items/d09709.pdf; Bureau of Alcohol, Tobacco, Firearms, and Explosives, "Mexico," Department of Justice, March 10, 2014, https://www.atf.gov/sites/default/files/assets/statistics/TraceData/TraceData_Intl/2013/mexico_-_cy08-13_atf_website.pdf.

97. Arindrajit Dube, Oeindrila Dube, and Omar Garcia-Ponce, "Cross-Border Spillover: U.S. Gun Laws and Violence in Mexico," American Political Science Review vol. 107, no. 3, August 2013, http://journals.cambridge.org/action/displayAbstract?fromPage=online&aid=8963077.

98. The RAND Corporation estimates that Mexico's drug revenues reach between $6.2 billion and $7.2 billion. The U.S. government has reported revenue totals of between $19 billion and $29 billion. Beau Kilmer, Jonathan P. Caulkins, Brittany M. Bond, and Peter H. Reuter, "Reducing Drug Trafficking Revenues and Violence in Mexico: Would Legalizing Marijuana in California Help?" RAND Corporation, 2010, http://www.rand.org/content/dam/rand/pubs/occasional_papers/2010/RAND_OP325.pdf; U.S. Department of Homeland Security, "United States of America-Mexico:

Bi-National Criminal Proceeds Study," June 2010, http://www.ice.gov/doclib/corner-stone/pdf/cps-study.pdf.

99. Office of Intelligence Warning, Plans, and Programs, "National Drug Threat Assessment Summary 2013," Drug Enforcement Administration, U.S. Department of Justice, November 2013, http://www.justice.gov/dea/resource-center/DIR-017-13%20NDTA%20Summary%20final.pdf; "Heroin Gains Popularity as Cheap Doses Flood the U.S.," *Time*, February 4, 2014, http://time.com/4505/heroin-gains-popularity-as-cheap-doses-flood-the-u-s.

100. Marijuana is the most popular drug, with 18.9 million Americans reporting that they used it in the past month. Some 6.8 million Americans abused prescription drugs in the same time period, 1.6 million reported using cocaine, 1.1 reported using hallucinogens, and much smaller numbers of Americans reported using inhalants and heroin. Substance Abuse and Mental Health Services Administration, "Results from the 2012 National Survey on Drug Use and Health: Summary of National Findings," U.S. Department of Health and Human Services, September 2013, http://www.samhsa.gov/data/NSDUH/2012SummNatFindDetTables/NationalFindings/NSDUHresults2012.htm#ch2.

101. United Nations Office on Drugs and Crime, "Homicide counts and rates, time series 2000–2012," accessed July 6, 2014, http://www.unodc.org/gsh/en/data.html.

102. The United States has one federal and four private icebreakers of at least ten thousand horsepower and has been talking about adding one additional icebreaker. Canada has six icebreakers and one planned (all are government owned). Russia, by contrast, has thirty-seven icebreakers that are either government- or privately owned, with four more under construction and eight more planned. USNI News, "U.S. Coast Guard's 2013 Review of Major Icebreakers of the World," July 24, 2013, http://news.usni.org/2013/07/23/u-s-coast-guards-2013-reivew-of-major-ice-breakers-of-the-world; Ronald O'Rourke, "Coast Guard Polar Icebreaker Modernization: Background and Issues for Congress," Congressional Research Service, March 28, 2014, https://www.fas.org/sgp/crs/weapons/RL34391.pdf.

103. Laura Dawson, Christopher Sands, and Duncan Wood, "North American Competitiveness: The San Diego Agenda," Dawson Strategic, Hudson Institute, and the Woodrow Wilson Center Mexico Institute, November 2013, http://www.wilsoncenter.org/sites/default/files/Working%20Together%20Full%20Document.pdf, p. 4.

104. Bureau of Transportation Statistics, "Border Crossing/Entry Data: Query Detailed Statistics," December 2013, http://transborder.bts.gov/programs/international/transborder/TBDR_BC/TBDR_BCQ.html.

105. Jeb Bush, Thomas F. McLarty III, and Edward Alden, *U.S. Immigration Policy*, Independent Task Force Report No. 63 (New York: Council on Foreign Relations Press, 2009), http://www.cfr.org/immigration/us-immigration-policy/p20030.

106. Jeffrey Passel, "Net Migration from Mexico Falls to Zero—and Perhaps Less," Pew Research Center, April 23, 2012, http://www.pewhispanic.org/files/2012/04/Mexican-migrants-report_final.pdf, p. 44; Aaron Terrazas, "Mexican Immigrants in the United States," Migration Policy Institute, February 22, 2010, http://www.migrationinformation.org/usfocus/display.cfm?ID=767.

107. Andrea Caumont, "Unauthorized Immigration," Pew Research Center, September 23, 2013, http://www.pewhispanic.org/2013/09/23/unauthorized-immigration; U.S. Census Bureau, "Current Population Survey Data on the Foreign-Born Population," accessed December 6, 2013, http://www.census.gov/population/foreign/data/cps.html.

108. Pew Research Center, "The Rise of Asian Americans," April 4, 2013, http://www.pewsocialtrends.org/2012/06/19/the-rise-of-asian-americans.

109. Instituto Nacional de Estadísticas y Geografía, "Conociendo . . . Nos Todos," May 2011,

http://www.inegi.org.mx/inegi/contenidos/espanol/prensa/contenidos/Articulos/sociodemograficas/nacidosenotropais.pdf.

110. Comisión Nacional de los Derechos Humanos, "Informe Especial Sobre Secuestro de Migrantes en México," February 22, 2011, http://www.cndh.org.mx/sites/all/fuentes/documentos/informes/especiales/2011_secmigrantes_0.pdf; Ernesto Rodríguez Chávez, Salvador Berumen Sandoval, and Luis Felipe Ramos, "Migración centroamericana de tránsito irregular por México. Estimaciones y características generales," Instituto Nacional de Migración, *Apuntes sobre Migración* no. 1, July 2011, http://www.gobernacion.gob.mx/work/models/SEGOB/Resource/2101/1/images/APUNTES_N1_Jul2011.pdf.

111. Linda Levine, "Immigration: The Effects on Low-Skilled and High-Skilled Native-Born Workers," Congressional Research Service, April 13, 2010, http://www.au.af.mil/au/awc/awcgate/crs/95-408.pdf, p. 7.

112. Michael Greenstone and Adam Looney, "Ten Economic Facts About Immigration," Hamilton Project, September 2010, http://www.hamiltonproject.org/files/downloads_and_links/09_immigration.pdf.

113. Robert Lynch and Patrick Oakland, "The Economic Effects of Granting Legal Status and Citizenship to Undocumented Immigrants," Center for American Progress, March 20, 2013, http://www.americanprogress.org/issues/immigration/report/2013/03/20/57351/the-economic-effects-of-granting-legal-status-and-citizenship-to-undocumented-immigrants.

114. Partnership for a New American Economy, "Open for Business: How Immigrants are Driving Small Business Creation in the United States," August 2012, http://www.renewoureconomy.org/sites/all/themes/pnae/ openforbusiness.pdf.

115. James P. Smith and Barry Edmonston, *The New Americans: Economic, Demographic, and Fiscal Effects of Immigration* (Washington, DC: National Research Council, National Academy of Sciences Press, 1997), pp. 220, 353.

116. Benjamin Page and Felix Reichling, "The Economic Impact of S. 744, the Border Security, Economic Opportunity, and Immigration Modernization Act," Congressional Budget Office, June 2013, http://www.cbo.gov/sites/default/files/cbofiles/attachments/44346-Immigration.pdf.

117. National Conference on State Legislatures, "States Pass 437 Immigration Laws and Resolutions in 2013," January 21, 2014, http://www.ncsl.org/press-room/states-pass-437-immigration-laws-and-resolutions-in-2013.aspx.

118. World Bank, "Fertility Rate, Total (Births per Woman) 2012," accessed December 6, 2013, http://data.worldbank.org/indicator/SP.DYN.TFRT.IN; Eurostat, "Total Fertility Rate 2012," European Commission, accessed December 6, 2013, http://epp.eurostat.ec.europa.eu/tgm/table.do?tab=table&init=1&plugin=1&language=en&pcode=tsdde220.

119. Organization for Economic Cooperation and Development, "PISA 2012 Results," accessed December 6, 2013, http://www.oecd.org/pisa/keyfindings/pisa-2012-results.htm.

120. World Economic Forum, "Practising Talent for Economic Growth," June 16, 2011, http://www.iom.int/jahia/webdav/shared/shared/mainsite/microsites/IDM/workshops/economic-cycles-demographic-change/Session-2-Anna-Janczak.pdf.

121. Derek Burleton, Sonya Gulati, Connor McDonald, and Sonny Scarfone, "Jobs in Canada, Where, What, and For Whom?" TD Economics, October 22, 2013, http://www.td.com/document/PDF/economics/special/JobsInCanada.pdf.

122. Office of the Vice President, "Statement on the U.S.-Mexico Bilateral Forum on Higher Education, Innovation, and Research," the White House, September 20, 2013, http://www.whitehouse.gov/the-press-office/2013/09/20/statement-us-mexico-bilateral-forum-higher-education-innovation-and-rese.

123. Institute of International Education, "Top 25 Places of Origin of International

Students, 2011/12-2012/13," accessed December 6, 2013, http://www.iie.org/Research-and-Publications/Open-Doors/Data/International-Students/Leading-Places-of-Origin/2011-13.

124. Institute of International Education, "Top 25 Destinations of U.S. Study Abroad Students, 2010/11-2011/12,"; Jon Marcus, "Canada Aims for US Student Growth," *Times Higher Education*, December 19, 2013, http://www.timeshighereducation.co.uk/news/canada-aims-for-us-student-growth/2009928.article.

125. U.S. Department of State, "Worldwide NIV Workload by Visa Category FY 2013," September 30, 2013, http://travel.state.gov/content/dam/visas/Statistics/Non-Immigrant-Statistics/NIVWorkload/FY2013NIVWorkloadbyVisaCategory.pdf.

126. Emily Loose, "U.S., Canada and Mexico Announce Cooperation on Wilderness," Wild Foundation, November 9, 2009, http://www.wild.org/blog/us-canada-and-mexico-announce-cooperation-on-wilderness.

127. Nicole T. Carter, Clare Ribando Seelke, and Daniel T. Shedd, "U.S.-Mexico Water Sharing: Background and Recent Developments," Congressional Research Service, November 19, 2013, http://www.fas.org/sgp/crs/row/R43312.pdf.

128. Stratfor, "The U.S., Mexico and the Decline of the Colorado River," *Forbes*, May 14, 2013, http://www.forbes.com/sites/stratfor/2013/05/14/u-s-mexico-the-decline-of-the-colorado-river.

129. Texas Commission on Environmental Quality, "Water Shortage Issue Related to the Mexican Water Deficit," August 12, 2014, http://www.tceq.state.tx.us/border/water-deficit.html.

130. Laurie Garrett, "Swine Flu: How the H1N1 Virus Got Its Start," *Newsweek*, May 1, 2009, http://www.newsweek.com/swine-flu-how-h1n1-virus-got-its-start-80117.

131. Pastor, *The North American Idea*.

132. U.S. Government Accountability Office, "U.S.-Mexico Border: CBP Action Needed to Improve Wait Time Data and Measure Outcomes of Trade Facilitation Efforts," July 24, 2013, http://www.gao.gov/products/GAO-13-603.

133. Bryan Roberts, Nathaniel Heatwole, Dan Wei, Misak Avetisyan, Oswin, Chan, Adam Rose, and Isaac Maya, "The Impact on the U.S. Economy of Changes in Wait Times at Ports of Entry," National Center for Risk and Economic Analysis of Terrorism Events, August 4, 2013, http://create.usc.edu/CBP%20Final%20Report.pdf.

134. U.S. Customs and Border Protection, "Meeting Land Port of Entry Modernization Needs in a Constrained Budgetary Environment," October 27–28, 2011, http://texasbmps.com/wp-content/uploads/downloads/2011/11/Pavlov_JWC-CBP-Presentation1.pdf.

135. This occurs within the Infrastructure Finance Unit in the Office of Technical Assistance. Heidi Crebo-Rediker, "Infrastructure Finance in America—How We Get Smarter," Council on Foreign Relations Press, March 2014, http://www.cfr.org/united-states/infrastructure-finance-america-we-get-smarter/p32597.

136. North American Development Bank, "Loan Program," accessed on June 20, 2014, http://www.nadbank.org/programs/loans.asp.

137. Kilmer, Caulkins, et. al., "Reducing Drug Trafficking Revenues and Violence in Mexico: Would Legalizing Marijuana in California Help?"

138. U.S. Office of National Drug Control Policy, "Cost Benefits of Investing Early In Substance Abuse Treatment," May 2012, http://www.whitehouse.gov/sites/default/files/ondcp/Fact_Sheets/investing_in_treatment_5-23-12.pdf.

139. U.S. Department of State, "Worldwide NIV Workload by Visa Category FY 2013," 2013, http://travel.state.gov/content/dam/visas/Statistics/Non-Immigrant-Statistics/NIVWorkload/FY2013NIVWorkloadbyVisaCategory.pdf.

Task Force Members

Bernard W. Aronson is a founding partner of ACON Investments, a middle-market private equity group with offices in Washington, DC; Los Angeles; Bogota; Mexico City; and São Paulo. Aronson previously served as an international adviser to Goldman Sachs & Co. from 1993 to 1996 and as assistant secretary of state for inter-American affairs from 1989 to 1993. In 1993, the secretary of state presented him with the Distinguished Service Award, the department's highest honor, for his role in ending the conflicts in Central America. He was previously deputy assistant to the president of the United States, executive speechwriter to the president, and special assistant and speechwriter to the vice president from 1977 to 1981. Aronson currently serves on the board of directors for Kate Spade Inc.; Royal Caribbean Cruise Lines, Inc.; Sequitur Energy; Chroma Oil and Gas; and ACON Franchise Holdings. He previously served as director of Hyatt Hotels Inc. He also serves on the board of directors of the National Democratic Institute for International Affairs, the Nature Conservancy Maryland/DC Chapter, and the Amazon Conservation Team. He graduated with honors from the University of Chicago and is a member of the Council on Foreign Relations.

Jodi Hanson Bond is vice president of the Americas for the International Division at the U.S. Chamber of Commerce. Her portfolio includes management of the Brazil-U.S. Business Council, the U.S.-Mexico Leadership Initiative, and the Association of American Chambers of Commerce in Latin America (AACCLA). Previously, Bond served as vice president of global government relations and country management for the Motorola Corporation. While at Motorola, she was regional director of country management for the Americas and Israel and managed advocacy teams across the globe. She was vice president of Fontheim International, where she advised *Fortune* 500 companies on global tax, energy, and corporate social responsibility matters. Bond was appointed deputy assistant secretary of the U.S. Department of Energy in 2001, during which time she served as the conduit for the U.S. secretary of energy and administrator of the National Nuclear Security Administration to the U.S. Congress. Bond holds a BA in politics from Whitman College and an MA in government from Johns Hopkins University. She also studied comparative and international politics at the University of London. Bond is an appointed member of Women Corporate Directors and the Economic Club of Washington, DC.

Robert C. Bonner is the senior principal of the Sentinel HS Group, LLC, a Washington, DC–based homeland security and data analytics consulting firm that provides strategic advice regarding homeland and border security issues and the use of automated data to identify risks. He is also a former partner of and currently counsel to Gibson, Dunn & Crutcher. Bonner served as the first commissioner of U.S. Customs and Border Protection, the agency of the Department of Homeland Security responsible for managing and securing the U.S. borders. Prior to that, he served as administrator of the Drug Enforcement Administration, commissioner of the U.S. Customs Service, a U.S. district judge, and the U.S. attorney for the Central District of California.

Jason Eric Bordoff joined the Columbia School of International and Public Affairs (SIPA) faculty after serving until January 2013 as special assistant to the president and senior director for energy and climate change on the staff of the National Security Council and, prior to that, holding senior positions on the National Economic Council and Council on Environmental Quality. At Columbia, he is a professor of professional practice and serves as founding director of the Center on Global Energy Policy. Previously, Bordoff was policy director of the Hamilton Project, an economic policy initiative housed at the Brookings Institution. During the Bill Clinton administration, he was an adviser to the deputy treasury secretary. Bordoff graduated with honors from Harvard Law School, where he was an editor of the *Harvard Law Review*, and clerked on the U.S. Court of Appeals for the DC Circuit. He also holds a BA magna cum laude and Phi Beta Kappa from Brown University and an MLitt from Oxford University, which he pursued as a Marshall scholar.

Timothy P. Daly is senior vice president of global public policy at Western Union, directing the company's government, political, and community affairs advocacy in two hundred countries and territories around the world. Prior to joining Western Union, Daly was at the Denver law firm Isaacson Rosenbaum, specializing in government advocacy, election law, and constitutional law. Daly also served as chief legal counsel and legislative director to Colorado governor Roy Romer. After Governor Romer's term, Daly served as vice president of legislative and political strategy for the telecommunications company US West. Daly received his law degree from George Washington University in 1988. During law school, he served as a legal clerk for Senator Tim Wirth (D-CO) and was the research assistant for Dean Jerome Barron and Professor Thomas Dienes. Daly earned degrees in political science and Spanish, with honors in political science, from San Diego State University. As an undergraduate, he was an intern at the Center for Strategic and International Studies. He was appointed by the governor to serve on the board of directors of Great Outdoors Colorado, chairing the local government committee. He also serves on the boards of the Woodrow Wilson Center for International Scholars Mexico Institute, the Public Affairs Council, and Jobs for America's Graduates.

Jorge I. Domínguez is the Antonio Madero professor for the study of Mexico at Harvard University. His most recent works include *Mexico's Evolving Democracy: A Comparative Study of the 2012 Elections* (Johns Hopkins University Press, forthcoming), edited by J. I. Domínguez, K. Greene, C. Lawson, and A. Moreno, and *The United States and Mexico: Between Partnership and Conflict* (with R. Fernández de Castro; Routledge, 2009). He has been a distinguished visiting professor at El Colegio de México and the Centro de Investigación y Docencia Económicas (CIDE). He is a member of the editorial board of *Foro Internacional* and *Foreign Affairs Latinoamérica*, headquartered in El Colegio de México and the Instituto Tecnológico Autónomo de México, respectively. At Harvard, he has been vice provost for international affairs, director of the Weatherhead Center for International Affairs, and chairman of the Harvard Academy for International and Area Studies. He has also served as president of the Latin American Studies Association.

Stephen E. Flynn is a professor of political science and the founding director of the Center for Resilience Studies at Northeastern University. Before arriving at Northeastern, he served as president of the Center for National Policy and spent a decade as a senior fellow for national security studies at the Council on Foreign Relations. In 2008, he served as the lead homeland security policy adviser for the presidential transition team for President Obama. He holds research affiliations with the Wharton School's Risk Management and Decision Processes Center, Columbia University's National Disaster Preparedness Center, and the Homeland Security Studies and Analysis Institute. Flynn was an active-duty commissioned officer in the U.S. Coast Guard for twenty years, including two tours as commanding officer at sea. He is the author of *The Edge of Disaster: Rebuilding a Resilient Nation* (Random House, 2007) and *America the Vulnerable* (HarperCollins, 2004). Flynn holds MALD and PhD degrees from Tufts University's Fletcher School of Law and Diplomacy.

Gordon D. Giffin is the chair of the public policy and international department of McKenna Long & Aldridge LLP. His practice focuses on international transactions and trade matters, government procurement, federal and state regulatory matters, and public policy. Giffin served as the nineteenth U.S. ambassador to Canada from 1997 to 2001 and was the recipient of the Distinguished Service Award from the Department of State in 1999. Between 1975 and 1979, Giffin was legislative director and chief counsel to U.S. senator Sam Nunn (D-GA). Giffin is currently a member of the Trilateral Commission; he also serves on the board of trustees of the Carter Presidential Center and on the board of directors of Canadian National Railway; Canadian Imperial Bank of Commerce; TransAlta, Inc.; Canadian Natural Resources Ltd.; and Element Financial Corp.

Neal R. Goins was named vice president of international government relations for Exxon Mobil Corporation in November 2013. Raised in Latin America, Goins received his undergraduate degree in physics from Princeton University in 1973 and a PhD in geophysics from the Massachusetts Institute of Technology in 1978 before joining Mobil Corporation that same year. Goins held various positions in research and development, operations, management, and corporate planning at

Mobil from 1978 to 1993. He managed Mobil's Nigerian exploration business from 1994 to 1997 and was the corporation's principal geoscientist from 1997 to 1999, with global responsibility for geoscience technology and project quality. After the merger of Exxon and Mobil, Goins served as a technical development manager from 1999 to 2002, manager of Nigerian exploration and new opportunity business from 2002 to 2005, and president of ExxonMobil Ventures Mexico from 2005 to 2009. Goins is a member of the U.S. Department of State advisory committee on economic policy, the U.S. Chamber of Commerce international policy committee, the USCIB executive committee, and the World Affairs Council of America national board and is a trustee of the Meridian International Center. He is the author of more than forty peer-reviewed papers on geoscience and holds four patents.

Kenneth I. Juster is a partner and managing director at the global private equity firm Warburg Pincus. He previously served in the U.S. government as undersecretary of commerce (2001–2005), acting counselor of the Department of State (1992–93), and deputy and senior adviser to Deputy Secretary of State Lawrence S. Eagleburger (1989–92). In the private sector, Juster has been executive vice president of Salesforce.com (2005–2010), a leading technology company that pioneered cloud computing for business enterprises, and a senior partner at the law firm Arnold & Porter (1981–89, 1993–2001), where he practiced international law. Juster is chairman of the advisory committee of Harvard's Weatherhead Center for International Affairs, chairman of the board of Freedom House, vice chairman of the board of the Asia Foundation, and a member of the Trilateral Commission, the Council on Foreign Relations, the American Academy of Diplomacy, and the international advisory board of the University of Pennsylvania's Center for the Advanced Study of India. He also served on the president's advisory committee for trade policy and negotiations from 2007 to 2010. Juster holds a BA in government from Harvard College, an MPP in public policy from the Harvard Kennedy School, and a JD from Harvard Law School.

Marie-Josée Kravis is an economist specializing in public policy analysis and strategic planning and was executive director of the Hudson Institute of Canada from 1976 to 1994. In 1994, she became a senior fellow of the Hudson Institute. Kravis is president of the Museum of Modern Art and chair of the Sloan Kettering Institute and vice chair of the board of trustees of the Hudson Institute. She is vice chair of the board of overseers and board of managers of Memorial Sloan Kettering Cancer Center. She is also a member of the international advisory committee of the Federal Reserve Bank of New York, the board of trustees of the Economic Club of New York, and the Council on Foreign Relations. Kravis was a member of the boards of directors of Ford Motor Company and InterActiveCorp and now serves on the boards of Publicis Groupe and LVMH. She is an international trustee of the Prado Museum. Kravis was made an officer of the Order of Canada and is an officier of the French Légion d'Honneur.

Jane Holl Lute is the president and chief executive officer of the Council on CyberSecurity. Lute most recently served as deputy secretary for the Department of Homeland Security, where she was responsible for day-to-day management of the department's efforts to prevent terrorism and enhance security, reinforce the nation's borders, administer and enforce U.S. immigration laws, strengthen national resilience in the face of disasters, and ensure the nation's cybersecurity. From 2003 to 2009, Lute served as assistant secretary-general of the United Nations, where she was responsible for providing comprehensive on-the-ground support to UN peace operations worldwide, and before that she served as assistant secretary-general for peacebuilding. Prior to joining the UN, Lute was executive vice president and chief operating officer of the United Nations Foundation and the Better World Fund. She worked with David A. Hamburg, former president of the Carnegie Corporation of New York, and Cyrus Vance, former U.S. secretary of state, on the Carnegie Commission on Preventing Deadly Conflict. Lute served on the National Security Council staff under Presidents George H.W. Bush and Bill Clinton and led a distinguished career in the U.S. Army, including service in the Persian Gulf during Operation Desert Storm. She holds a PhD in political science from Stanford University and a JD from Georgetown Law.

Jason Marczak is deputy director of the Adrienne Arsht Latin America Center at the Atlantic Council. He joined the Atlantic Council in October 2013 to help launch the Arsht Center and set the strategic direction for its Latin America work. Marczak previously served as director of policy at Americas Society / Council of the Americas (AS/COA) in New York City, where he was a cofounder and senior editor of *Americas Quarterly*. Prior to joining AS/COA in 2006, Marczak was a program officer and founding member of Partners of the Americas' Center for Civil Society. From 1999 to 2001, he was a legislative aide for Congressman Sam Farr (D-CA). He has also worked at the National Endowment for Democracy and the Andean Community General Secretariat in Lima, Peru. Marczak is a frequent commentator on political and economic issues in Latin America, including a weekly appearance on Bloomberg TV in Mexico. He has written for such outlets as CNN, the *Financial Times*, and *Foreign Affairs*, as well as *El Universal*, *El País*, and *O Estado de São Paulo*. He received a BA from Tufts University and an MA from the Johns Hopkins University School of Advanced International Studies (SAIS). Marczak is a term member of the Council on Foreign Relations.

Diana Natalicio was named president of the University of Texas at El Paso (UTEP) in 1988, where she also served as vice president for academic affairs, dean of liberal arts, and chair of modern languages. During her twenty-five-year tenure, UTEP's enrollment has grown from fifteen thousand to twenty-three thousand students, its annual budget from $65 million to more than $400 million, annual research expenditures from $6 million to more than $84 million, and number of doctoral programs from one to twenty. Natalicio was most recently chair of the board of the American Council on Education. She has served as a trustee of the Rockefeller Foundation, member and vice chair of the National Science Board, and board member of the Association of Public and Land-Grant Universities, Trinity Industries, the U.S.-Mexico Foundation for Science, Sandia Corporation, and Internet2. Natalicio has received numerous honors and awards, including honorary doctoral degrees from Georgetown University, Smith College, and Universidad Autónoma de Nuevo Leon. In 2011, she was awarded the Orden Mexicana del Aguila Azteca, the highest honor bestowed on foreign nationals by the president of Mexico.

Shannon K. O'Neil is senior fellow for Latin America studies at the Council on Foreign Relations. Her expertise includes U.S.-Latin America relations, trade, energy, and immigration. She is the author of *Two Nations Indivisible: Mexico, the United States, and the Road Ahead* (Oxford University Press, 2013). O'Neil has testified before Congress on U.S. policy toward Mexico, has spoken at numerous conferences, and is a frequent commentator on major television and radio programs. Her work has been published in *Foreign Affairs, Foreign Affairs Latinoamerica, Americas Quarterly, Política Exterior, Foreign Policy*, the *Washington Post*, the *Los Angeles Times*, and *USA Today*, among others. Her blog, *Latin America's Moment*, analyzes developments in Latin America and U.S. relations in the region. O'Neil has lived and worked in Mexico and Argentina and travels extensively in Latin America. She was a Fulbright scholar; a justice, welfare, and economics fellow at Harvard University; and a professor of Latin American politics at Columbia University. Before turning to policy, O'Neil worked in the private sector as an equity analyst at Indosuez Capital and Credit Lyonnais Securities. She holds a BA from Yale University, an MA in international relations from Yale University, and a PhD in government from Harvard University.

Maria Otero served as undersecretary of state for civilian security, democracy, and human rights from 2009 to 2013, overseeing U.S. civilian security issues including democracy, human rights, refugees, trafficking in persons, counternarcotics, conflict prevention and response, and countering violent extremism. She also served as President Obama's special representative for Tibetan issues. Born in Bolivia, Otero was the highest ranking Hispanic official at the State Department and the first Latina undersecretary in its history. Otero currently serves as trustee at the Kresge Foundation; the Public Welfare Foundation; Development Alternatives Inc.; BancoSol, a microfinance bank in Bolivia; and Herbalife, a publicly traded U.S. company. Otero was formerly the president and chief executive officer of Accion (2000–2009), where she held other positions for twelve years. She was an adjunct professor at the Johns Hopkins University School of Advanced International Studies (SAIS) from 1998 to 2008. Otero served on the board of the U.S. Institute of Peace from 2000 to 2008, where was board vice chair. In 2006, UN secretary-general Kofi Annan appointed Otero to the UN Advisors Group on Inclusive Financial Sectors. Otero holds an MA in literature from the University of Maryland, an MA in international relations from SAIS, and an honorary doctorate of humane letters from Dartmouth College.

James W. Owens served as chairman and chief executive officer of Caterpillar Inc. in Peoria, Illinois, from 2004 through June 2010. Owens retired in mid-2010 after thirty-eight years of service at the company. He was president of Solar Turbines in San Diego from 1990–93 and corporate chief financial officer from 1993–95. In 1995, he became a group president and member of Caterpillar's executive office. While chairman, Owens served on the executive committee of the Business Roundtable, was chairman of the Business Council, and was an adviser to Presidents George W. Bush and Barack Obama. Owens is currently a director of Alcoa Inc., IBM Corporation, and Morgan Stanley. He also serves as a senior adviser to Kohlberg Kravis Roberts & Co. Owens is chairman of the executive committee for the Peterson Institute for International Economics and served on the Board of Directors of the Council on Foreign Relations. He served on the executive committee of the Business Council and was a member of President Obama's Economic Recovery Advisory Board from 2009 to 2010. He is also a member of the board of trustees for North Carolina State University in Raleigh, North Carolina. Owens is a native of Elizabeth City, North Carolina, and graduated from North Carolina State University in 1973 with a PhD in economics.

David H. Petraeus (U.S. Army, retired) is the chairman of the KKR Global Institute, a visiting professor of public policy at the City University of New York's Macaulay Honors College, a Judge Widney professor at the University of Southern California, a senior fellow at Harvard University, and a member of the advisory boards of six veterans organizations. Petraeus previously served thirty-seven years in the U.S. military, including as commander of coalition forces during the surges in both Iraq and Afghanistan and as commander of the U.S. Central Command. Following retirement from the military in August 2011, he served as director of the Central Intelligence Agency. Petraeus was a distinguished graduate of the U.S. Military Academy and earned MPA and PhD degrees in international relations from Princeton University.

Adrean Scheid Rothkopf is vice president of government relations, Latin America, for Millicom, a leading telecommunications and media company dedicated to emerging markets in Latin America and Africa.

Rothkopf is responsible for developing and executing policy and advocacy strategies for the region and coordinating outreach across markets. She works closely with other senior management to support the business objectives of Millicom by monitoring and influencing relevant legislation, regulation, and policy. She coordinates with senior government officials from the hemisphere and globally and participates actively in the work of industry associations and multilateral organizations to help advance the development of sound policies and practices that will ensure growth and competitiveness in the region. Prior to joining Millicom, Rothkopf was senior director of government relations, Latin America, for BlackBerry. Formerly, she was vice president of Western Hemisphere affairs at the U.S. Chamber of Commerce, where she led the activities of the department and served as executive vice president of the Association of American Chambers of Commerce in Latin America (AACCLA) and of the Brazil-U.S. Business Council. Earlier in her career, Rothkopf worked with the Group of Fifty, the Newmarket Company, the Inter-American Dialogue, the Council of the Americas, and the Carter Center.

Clifford M. Sobel served as ambassador to the Netherlands and Brazil throughout the George W. Bush and Obama administrations. Sobel has received awards from Brazil's ministry of defense and the state governments of Minas Gerais, Pernambuco, and Sergipe in recognition of his contributions to bilateral relations. He is currently managing partner of Valor Capital Group, a diversified investment group with significant investments in Brazil. He is also a partner of Related Brazil, a mixed-use developer in Brazil, and a partner and board member of Contagalo, a diversified agriculture group. He has served on advisory boards to the American Military Commander of Europe and NATO, as well as to the Command for American Forces for Central and South America. Sobel sits on the board of directors for Diamond Offshore Drilling, the Council of American Ambassadors, and the Council of the Americas, as well as on Christie's advisory board for the Americas. He serves on the board of Wenzhou Kean University based in Zhejiang Province, China, one of the first universities to grant degrees in English in accounting, finance, English, and computer science. He is also on the advisory board of Fundacao Dom Cabral Brazil (FDC), a leading school for executive education in Brazil.

James S. Taylor is an adviser and strategist for leaders, companies, and causes in the United States and Mexico. During the past twenty-five years, he has created and grown a number of successful companies in both countries. Today, Taylor serves as a founding partner of Vianovo, a management consultancy that specializes in high-stakes brand, policy, and crisis issues. At Vianovo, he co-chairs the firm's Mexico Energy Strategic Advisory (MESA) practice and also leads Vianovo Ventures, which partners with startups and investors. Taylor grew up in Mexico, and his early career focused on politics and trade. He worked for U.S. senator Lloyd Bentsen (D-TX) and later went on to advise Mexico's trade-negotiating team on building support to secure the passage of NAFTA. Taylor has been a regular contributor to Univision, and his pieces on Mexico's economic and political transformation and the U.S.-Mexico relationship have been featured in the *Dallas Morning News* and *National Journal.*

Robert B. Zoellick is chairman of Goldman Sachs's International Advisers. He serves on the boards of Temasek, Singapore's sovereign wealth fund, and Laureate International Universities. Zoellick is also a senior fellow at the Belfer Center at the Harvard Kennedy School. He is a board member of the congressionally founded National Endowment for Democracy and the Peterson Institute for International Economics. Zoellick was the president of the World Bank Group from 2007 to 2012. He served in President George W. Bush's Cabinet as U.S. trade representative from 2001 to 2005 and as deputy secretary of state from 2005 to 2006. From 1985 to 1993, Zoellick worked in the Treasury and State Departments in various capacities, including as counselor to the secretary of the treasury and undersecretary of state, as well as briefly in the White House as deputy chief of staff. Zoellick holds a BA (Phi Beta Kappa) from Swarthmore College, an MPP in public policy from the Harvard Kennedy School, and a JD magna cum laude from Harvard Law School.

Task Force Observers

Edward Alden is the Bernard L. Schwartz senior fellow at the Council on Foreign Relations in Washington, DC, and author of *The Closing of the American Border: Terrorism, Immigration and Security Since 9/11* (Harper Collins, 2008). He was project director for the CFR-sponsored Independent Task Force on U.S. Trade and Investment Policy (2011) and for the Independent Task Force on U.S. Immigration Policy (2009). He is also the director of CFR's Renewing America publication series. Most recently, he was coauthor of the CFR Working Paper *Managing Illegal Immigration to the United States: How Effective is Enforcement?* Prior to joining CFR in 2007, Alden was the Washington bureau chief for the *Financial Times.* He has written extensively about the U.S. response to globalization, focusing particularly on international trade, immigration, and homeland security. He has won several national and international awards for his writing and has written commentary for the *New York Times, Washington Post, Wall Street Journal, Los Angeles Times,* and many other magazines, newspapers, and websites. He lives in Bethesda, Maryland, with his wife and two children.

Christian Brose is senior policy adviser to Senator John McCain (R-AZ). He serves as the senator's top adviser on all national security, foreign policy, trade, and intelligence issues and supports the senator in his work as a member of the Senate Armed Services Committee and the Senate Foreign Relations Committee. He has accompanied McCain on his official travel to more than sixty countries. From 2008 to 2009, he was senior editor of *Foreign Policy* magazine. From 2005 to 2008, he served as policy adviser and chief speechwriter to Secretary of State Condoleezza Rice, working as a member of the secretary's policy planning staff. From 2004 to 2005, he was a junior speechwriter for Secretary of State Colin Powell. He has a BA in political science from Kenyon College and an MA from the Johns Hopkins University's School of Advanced International Studies, where he concentrated in international economics.

Thomas E. Donilon is vice chair of the international law firm of O'Melveny & Myers, where he serves on the firm's global governing committee. Donilon is also senior director at the BlackRock Investment Institute. From 2010 to 2013, he served as national security adviser to President Barack Obama. In that capacity, Donilon oversaw the National Security Council staff, chaired the cabinet-level National Security Principals Committee, provided the president's daily national security briefing, and was responsible for the coordination and integration of the U.S. government's foreign policy. He previously served as assistant to the president and principal deputy national security adviser. Donilon is a distinguished fellow at the Council on Foreign Relations, a nonresident senior fellow at the Harvard Kennedy School's Belfer Center for Science and International Affairs, and a member of the U.S. Defense Policy Board and the Central Intelligence Agency's External Advisory Board. Donilon has worked closely with and advised three U.S. presidents since his first position at the White House in 1977, working with President Jimmy Carter. During the Clinton administration, he served as assistant secretary of state and chief of staff at the U.S. Department of State.

Juan Sebastian Gonzalez is special adviser to Vice President Joe Biden on Western Hemisphere affairs. Gonzalez was previously National Security Council staff director for the Andes from 2011 to 2013, where he advised the president's national security adviser and deputy national security adviser on matters related to U.S. policy in the Andean region. Before joining the White House, Gonzalez held various positions in the U.S. Department of State's Bureau of Western Hemisphere Affairs, including chief of staff to Assistant Secretary Arturo Valenzuela from 2009 to 2011, policy planning officer from 2007 to 2009, staff assistant to Assistant Secretary Thomas A. Shannon from 2006 to 2007, and Colombia desk officer from 2004 to 2006. Gonzalez was the recipient of numerous superior and meritorious honor awards during his time with the Department of State. From 2001 to 2004, Gonzalez served as a Peace Corps volunteer in Guatemala, and from 1998 to 2000 he served as legislative assistant to New York State assemblyman Sam Hoyt (D-144). He received a BS from the State University of New York, Buffalo, and an MA with distinction from Georgetown University's Edmund A. Walsh School of Foreign Service. He is a term member of the Council on Foreign Relations and speaks fluent Spanish. He is a native of Cartagena, Colombia.

Michael A. Levi is the David M. Rubenstein senior fellow for energy and the environment at the Council on Foreign Relations and director of CFR's Maurice R. Greenberg Center for Geoeconomic Studies. He is an expert on domestic and international energy markets and policy, climate change, and nuclear security. Levi is the author of four books, most recently *The Power Surge: Energy, Opportunity, and the Battle for America's Future* (Oxford University Press, 2013), which explored the drivers and consequences of two emerging revolutions in American energy, and *By All Means Necessary: How China's Resource Quest is Changing the World* (with Elizabeth Economy; Oxford University Press, 2014), which investigated Chinese efforts to secure natural resources, including in North America. His recent writings include studies of U.S. natural gas exports, the Canadian oil sands, and the global politics and economics of clean energy innovation. He is a member of the advisory board to Princeton University's Carbon Mitigation Initiative and a member of the strategic advisory board for NewWorld Capital Group LLC. Before joining CFR, Levi was a science fellow in foreign policy studies at the Brookings Institution. Levi holds an MA in physics from Princeton University and a PhD in war studies from the University of London (King's College).

Matthew Padilla is Senator Tom Udall's military and foreign relations legislative assistant. He advises Senator Udall on issues pertaining to national security, foreign policy, and veterans' issues, and he recently completed the Woodrow Wilson Center foreign policy fellowship. He received his BA in political science with a concentration in international relations from the University of Notre Dame. On graduation, he was commissioned an ensign (O-1) in the U.S. Navy through Notre Dame's Naval Reserve Officers' Training Corps (NROTC). He served in the U.S. Navy as a surface warfare officer aboard the USS *Iwo Jima* (LHD-7), and the USS *Laboon* (DDG-58) from 2003 to 2007. Following his active-duty service, he received his JD from American University Washington College of Law. He is a native of Albuquerque, New Mexico, and a member of the State Bar of New Mexico.

Vance Serchuk is executive director of the KKR Global Institute. He is an adjunct senior fellow at the Center for a New American Security in Washington, DC, and a lecturer of law at Columbia Law School. He was previously senior foreign policy adviser to Senator Joseph

Lieberman (I-CT) for six years, and a professional staff member on the Senate Homeland Security and Governmental Affairs Committee. During the first half of 2013, he was a CFR international affairs fellow, based in Japan, and a monthly foreign affairs columnist for the *Washington Post*. His writings have appeared in the *New York Times, Wall Street Journal, Los Angeles Times, Weekly Standard,* and other publications. He is a summa cum laude graduate of Princeton University, holds a JD from Yale Law School, and was a Fulbright scholar in the Russian Federation.

Julia E. Sweig is the Nelson and David Rockefeller senior fellow for Latin America studies and director for Latin America studies at the Council on Foreign Relations. Sweig also directs CFR's Global Brazil initiative. Sweig writes a biweekly column for *Folha de São Paulo,* Brazil's leading newspaper, and is the author of *Cuba: What Everyone Needs to Know* (Oxford University Press, 2009) and *Friendly Fire: Losing Friends and Making Enemies in the Anti-American Century* (PublicAffairs, 2006), as well as numerous publications on Latin America and American foreign policy. Sweig's *Inside the Cuban Revolution: Fidel Castro and the Urban Underground* (Harvard University Press, 2002) received the American Historical Association's Herbert Feis Award for best book of the year by an independent scholar. Sweig serves on the international advisory board of the Brazilian Center for International Relations (CEBRI). She was the Sol M. Linowitz professor of international relations at Hamilton College in 2011 and, from 1999 to 2008, served as a consultant on Latin American affairs for the Aspen Institute's congressional program. She holds a BA from the University of California and an MA and a PhD from the Johns Hopkins University School of Advanced International Studies (SAIS).

Independent Task Force Reports

Published by the Council on Foreign Relations

Defending an Open, Global, Secure, and Resilient Internet
John D. Negroponte and Samuel J. Palmisano, *Chairs*; Adam Segal, *Project Director*
Independent Task Force Report No. 70 (2013)

U.S.-Turkey Relations: A New Partnership
Madeleine K. Albright and Stephen J. Hadley, Chairs; Steven A. Cook, Project Director
Independent Task Force Report No. 69 (2012)

U.S. Education Reform and National Security
Joel I. Klein and Condoleezza Rice, Chairs; Julia Levy, Project Director
Independent Task Force Report No. 68 (2012)

U.S. Trade and Investment Policy
Andrew H. Card and Thomas A. Daschle, Chairs; Edward Alden and Matthew J. Slaughter,
Project Directors
Independent Task Force Report No. 67 (2011)

Global Brazil and U.S.-Brazil Relations
Samuel W. Bodman and James D. Wolfensohn, Chairs; Julia E. Sweig, Project Director
Independent Task Force Report No. 66 (2011)

U.S. Strategy for Pakistan and Afghanistan
Richard L. Armitage and Samuel R. Berger, Chairs; Daniel S. Markey, Project Director
Independent Task Force Report No. 65 (2010)

U.S. Policy Toward the Korean Peninsula
Charles L. Pritchard and John H. Tilelli Jr., Chairs; Scott A. Snyder, Project Director
Independent Task Force Report No. 64 (2010)

U.S. Immigration Policy
Jeb Bush and Thomas F. McLarty III, Chairs; Edward Alden, Project Director
Independent Task Force Report No. 63 (2009)

U.S. Nuclear Weapons Policy
William J. Perry and Brent Scowcroft, Chairs; Charles D. Ferguson, Project Director
Independent Task Force Report No. 62 (2009)

Confronting Climate Change: A Strategy for U.S. Foreign Policy
George E. Pataki and Thomas J. Vilsack, Chairs; Michael A. Levi, Project Director
Independent Task Force Report No. 61 (2008)

U.S.-Latin America Relations: A New Direction for a New Reality
Charlene Barshefsky and James T. Hill, Chairs; Shannon O'Neil, Project Director
Independent Task Force Report No. 60 (2008)

U.S.-China Relations: An Affirmative Agenda, A Responsible Course
Carla A. Hills and Dennis C. Blair, Chairs; Frank Sampson Jannuzi, Project Director
Independent Task Force Report No. 59 (2007)

National Security Consequences of U.S. Oil Dependency
John Deutch and James R. Schlesinger, Chairs; David G. Victor, Project Director
Independent Task Force Report No. 58 (2006)

Russia's Wrong Direction: What the United States Can and Should Do
John Edwards and Jack Kemp, Chairs; Stephen Sestanovich, Project Director
Independent Task Force Report No. 57 (2006)

More than Humanitarianism: A Strategic U.S. Approach Toward Africa
Anthony Lake and Christine Todd Whitman, Chairs; Princeton N. Lyman and J. Stephen Morrison, Project Directors
Independent Task Force Report No. 56 (2006)

In the Wake of War: Improving Post-Conflict Capabilities
Samuel R. Berger and Brent Scowcroft, Chairs; William L. Nash, Project Director; Mona K. Sutphen, Deputy Director
Independent Task Force Report No. 55 (2005)

In Support of Arab Democracy: Why and How
Madeleine K. Albright and Vin Weber, Chairs; Steven A. Cook, Project Director
Independent Task Force Report No. 54 (2005)

Building a North American Community
John P. Manley, Pedro Aspe, and William F. Weld, Chairs; Thomas d'Aquino, Andrés Rozental, and Robert Pastor, Vice Chairs; Chappell H. Lawson, Project Director
Independent Task Force Report No. 53 (2005)

Iran: Time for a New Approach
Zbigniew Brzezinski and Robert M. Gates, Chairs; Suzanne Maloney, Project Director
Independent Task Force Report No. 52 (2004)

An Update on the Global Campaign Against Terrorist Financing
Maurice R. Greenberg, Chair; William F. Wechsler and Lee S. Wolosky, Project Directors
Independent Task Force Report No. 40B (Web-only release, 2004)

Renewing the Atlantic Partnership
Henry A. Kissinger and Lawrence H. Summers, Chairs; Charles A. Kupchan, Project Director
Independent Task Force Report No. 51 (2004)

Iraq: One Year After
Thomas R. Pickering and James R. Schlesinger, Chairs; Eric P. Schwartz, Project Consultant
Independent Task Force Report No. 43C (Web-only release, 2004)

Nonlethal Weapons and Capabilities
Paul X. Kelley and Graham Allison, Chairs; Richard L. Garwin, Project Director
Independent Task Force Report No. 50 (2004)

New Priorities in South Asia: U.S. Policy Toward India, Pakistan, and Afghanistan
(Chairmen's Report)
Marshall Bouton, Nicholas Platt, and Frank G. Wisner, Chairs; Dennis Kux and Mahnaz
Ispahani, Project Directors
Independent Task Force Report No. 49 (2003)
Cosponsored with the Asia Society

Finding America's Voice: A Strategy for Reinvigorating U.S. Public Diplomacy
Peter G. Peterson, Chair; Kathy Bloomgarden, Henry Grunwald, David E. Morey, and
Shibley Telhami, Working Committee Chairs; Jennifer Sieg, Project Director; Sharon
Herbstman, Project Coordinator
Independent Task Force Report No. 48 (2003)

Emergency Responders: Drastically Underfunded, Dangerously Unprepared
Warren B. Rudman, Chair; Richard A. Clarke, Senior Adviser; Jamie F. Metzl,
Project Director
Independent Task Force Report No. 47 (2003)

Iraq: The Day After (Chairs' Update)
Thomas R. Pickering and James R. Schlesinger, Chairs; Eric P. Schwartz, Project Director
Independent Task Force Report No. 43B (Web-only release, 2003)

Burma: Time for Change
Mathea Falco, Chair
Independent Task Force Report No. 46 (2003)

Afghanistan: Are We Losing the Peace?
Marshall Bouton, Nicholas Platt, and Frank G. Wisner, Chairs; Dennis Kux and Mahnaz
Ispahani, Project Directors
Chairman's Report of an Independent Task Force (2003)
Cosponsored with the Asia Society

Meeting the North Korean Nuclear Challenge
Morton I. Abramowitz and James T. Laney, Chairs; Eric Heginbotham, Project Director
Independent Task Force Report No. 45 (2003)

Chinese Military Power
Harold Brown, Chair; Joseph W. Prueher, Vice Chair; Adam Segal, Project Director
Independent Task Force Report No. 44 (2003)

Iraq: The Day After
Thomas R. Pickering and James R. Schlesinger, Chairs; Eric P. Schwartz, Project Director
Independent Task Force Report No. 43 (2003)

Threats to Democracy: Prevention and Response
Madeleine K. Albright and Bronislaw Geremek, Chairs; Morton H. Halperin, Director;
Elizabeth Frawley Bagley, Associate Director
Independent Task Force Report No. 42 (2002)

America—Still Unprepared, Still in Danger
Gary Hart and Warren B. Rudman, Chairs; Stephen E. Flynn, Project Director
Independent Task Force Report No. 41 (2002)

Terrorist Financing
Maurice R. Greenberg, Chair; William F. Wechsler and Lee S. Wolosky, Project Directors
Independent Task Force Report No. 40 (2002)

Enhancing U.S. Leadership at the United Nations
David Dreier and Lee H. Hamilton, Chairs; Lee Feinstein and Adrian Karatnycky, Project Directors
Independent Task Force Report No. 39 (2002)
Cosponsored with Freedom House

Improving the U.S. Public Diplomacy Campaign in the War Against Terrorism
Carla A. Hills and Richard C. Holbrooke, Chairs; Charles G. Boyd, Project Director
Independent Task Force Report No. 38 (Web-only release, 2001)

Building Support for More Open Trade
Kenneth M. Duberstein and Robert E. Rubin, Chairs; Timothy F. Geithner, Project Director;
Daniel R. Lucich, Deputy Project Director
Independent Task Force Report No. 37 (2001)

Beginning the Journey: China, the United States, and the WTO
Robert D. Hormats, Chair; Elizabeth Economy and Kevin Nealer, Project Directors
Independent Task Force Report No. 36 (2001)

Strategic Energy Policy Update
Edward L. Morse, Chair; Amy Myers Jaffe, Project Director
Independent Task Force Report No. 33B (2001)
Cosponsored with the James A. Baker III Institute for Public Policy of Rice University

Testing North Korea: The Next Stage in U.S. and ROK Policy
Morton I. Abramowitz and James T. Laney, Chairs; Robert A. Manning, Project Director
Independent Task Force Report No. 35 (2001)

The United States and Southeast Asia: A Policy Agenda for the New Administration
J. Robert Kerrey, Chair; Robert A. Manning, Project Director
Independent Task Force Report No. 34 (2001)

Strategic Energy Policy: Challenges for the 21st Century
Edward L. Morse, Chair; Amy Myers Jaffe, Project Director
Independent Task Force Report No. 33 (2001)
Cosponsored with the James A. Baker III Institute for Public Policy of Rice University

A Letter to the President and a Memorandum on U.S. Policy Toward Brazil
Stephen Robert, Chair; Kenneth Maxwell, Project Director
Independent Task Force Report No. 32 (2001)

State Department Reform
Frank C. Carlucci, Chair; Ian J. Brzezinski, Project Coordinator
Independent Task Force Report No. 31 (2001)
Cosponsored with the Center for Strategic and International Studies

U.S.-Cuban Relations in the 21st Century: A Follow-on Report
Bernard W. Aronson and William D. Rogers, Chairs; Julia Sweig and Walter Mead, Project Directors
Independent Task Force Report No. 30 (2000)

Toward Greater Peace and Security in Colombia: Forging a Constructive U.S. Policy
Bob Graham and Brent Scowcroft, Chairs; Michael Shifter, Project Director
Independent Task Force Report No. 29 (2000)
Cosponsored with the Inter-American Dialogue

Future Directions for U.S. Economic Policy Toward Japan
Laura D'Andrea Tyson, Chair; M. Diana Helweg Newton, Project Director
Independent Task Force Report No. 28 (2000)

First Steps Toward a Constructive U.S. Policy in Colombia
Bob Graham and Brent Scowcroft, Chairs; Michael Shifter, Project Director
Interim Report (2000)
Cosponsored with the Inter-American Dialogue

Promoting Sustainable Economies in the Balkans
Steven Rattner, Chair; Michael B.G. Froman, Project Director
Independent Task Force Report No. 27 (2000)

Non-Lethal Technologies: Progress and Prospects
Richard L. Garwin, Chair; W. Montague Winfield, Project Director
Independent Task Force Report No. 26 (1999)

Safeguarding Prosperity in a Global Financial System:
The Future International Financial Architecture
Carla A. Hills and Peter G. Peterson, Chairs; Morris Goldstein, Project Director
Independent Task Force Report No. 25 (1999)
Cosponsored with the International Institute for Economics

U.S. Policy Toward North Korea: Next Steps
Morton I. Abramowitz and James T. Laney, Chairs; Michael J. Green, Project Director
Independent Task Force Report No. 24 (1999)

Reconstructing the Balkans
Morton I. Abramowitz and Albert Fishlow, Chairs; Charles A. Kupchan, Project Director
Independent Task Force Report No. 23 (Web-only release, 1999)

Strengthening Palestinian Public Institutions
Michel Rocard, Chair; Henry Siegman, Project Director; Yezid Sayigh and Khalil Shikaki, Principal Authors
Independent Task Force Report No. 22 (1999)

U.S. Policy Toward Northeastern Europe
Zbigniew Brzezinski, Chair; F. Stephen Larrabee, Project Director
Independent Task Force Report No. 21 (1999)

The Future of Transatlantic Relations
Robert D. Blackwill, Chair and Project Director
Independent Task Force Report No. 20 (1999)

U.S.-Cuban Relations in the 21st Century
Bernard W. Aronson and William D. Rogers, Chairs; Walter Russell Mead, Project Director
Independent Task Force Report No. 19 (1999)

After the Tests: U.S. Policy Toward India and Pakistan
Richard N. Haass and Morton H. Halperin, Chairs
Independent Task Force Report No. 18 (1998)
Cosponsored with the Brookings Institution

Managing Change on the Korean Peninsula
Morton I. Abramowitz and James T. Laney, Chairs; Michael J. Green, Project Director
Independent Task Force Report No. 17 (1998)

Promoting U.S. Economic Relations with Africa
Peggy Dulany and Frank Savage, Chairs; Salih Booker, Project Director
Independent Task Force Report No. 16 (1998)

U.S. Middle East Policy and the Peace Process
Henry Siegman, Project Coordinator
Independent Task Force Report No. 15 (1997)

Differentiated Containment: U.S. Policy Toward Iran and Iraq
Zbigniew Brzezinski and Brent Scowcroft, Chairs; Richard W. Murphy, Project Director
Independent Task Force Report No. 14 (1997)

Russia, Its Neighbors, and an Enlarging NATO
Richard G. Lugar, Chair; Victoria Nuland, Project Director
Independent Task Force Report No. 13 (1997)

Rethinking International Drug Control: New Directions for U.S. Policy
Mathea Falco, Chair
Independent Task Force Report No. 12 (1997)

Financing America's Leadership: Protecting American Interests and Promoting American Values
Mickey Edwards and Stephen J. Solarz, Chairs; Morton H. Halperin, Lawrence J. Korb,
and Richard M. Moose, Project Directors
Independent Task Force Report No. 11 (1997)
Cosponsored with the Brookings Institution

A New U.S. Policy Toward India and Pakistan
Richard N. Haass, Chair; Gideon Rose, Project Director
Independent Task Force Report No. 10 (1997)

Arms Control and the U.S.-Russian Relationship
Robert D. Blackwill, Chair and Author; Keith W. Dayton, Project Director
Independent Task Force Report No. 9 (1996)
Cosponsored with the Nixon Center for Peace and Freedom

American National Interest and the United Nations
George Soros, Chair
Independent Task Force Report No. 8 (1996)

Making Intelligence Smarter: The Future of U.S. Intelligence
Maurice R. Greenberg, Chair; Richard N. Haass, Project Director
Independent Task Force Report No. 7 (1996)

Lessons of the Mexican Peso Crisis
John C. Whitehead, Chair; Marie-Josée Kravis, Project Director
Independent Task Force Report No. 6 (1996)

Managing the Taiwan Issue: Key Is Better U.S. Relations with China
Stephen Friedman, Chair; Elizabeth Economy, Project Director
Independent Task Force Report No. 5 (1995)

Non-Lethal Technologies: Military Options and Implications
Malcolm H. Wiener, Chair
Independent Task Force Report No. 4 (1995)

Should NATO Expand?
Harold Brown, Chair; Charles A. Kupchan, Project Director
Independent Task Force Report No. 3 (1995)

Success or Sellout? The U.S.-North Korean Nuclear Accord
Kyung Won Kim and Nicholas Platt, Chairs; Richard N. Haass, Project Director
Independent Task Force Report No. 2 (1995)
Cosponsored with the Seoul Forum for International Affairs

Nuclear Proliferation: Confronting the New Challenges
Stephen J. Hadley, Chair; Mitchell B. Reiss, Project Director
Independent Task Force Report No. 1 (1995)

Note: Task Force reports are available for download from CFR's website, www.cfr.org.
For more information, email publications@cfr.org.